GASTON BACHELARD

On Poetic Imagination and Reverie

Selected, translated, and introduced by

Colette Gaudin

SPRING PUBLICATIONS

PUTNAM, CONN.

ISBN: 978-0-88214-331-6

Library of Congress Control Number: 87023314

CONTENTS

SOURCES

AS = L'Air et les songes: Essai sur l'imagination du mouvement (Paris: José Corti, 1943).

ER = L'Eau et les rêves: Essai sur l'imagination de la matière (Paris: José Corti, 1942).

FC = La Flamme d'une chandelle (Paris: Presses Universitaires de France, 1961).

FES = La Formation de l'esprit scientifique: Contribution à une psychanalyse de la connaissance objective (Paris: Vrin, 1938).

L = Lautréamont (Paris: José Corti, 1939).

PF = La Psychanalyse du feu (Paris: Gallimard, 1938).

PN = La Philosophie du "non": Essai d'une philosophie du nouvel esprit scientifique (Paris: Presses Universitaires de France, 1940).

PR = La Poétique de la rêverie (Paris: Presses Universitaires de France, 1960).

PE = La Poétique de l'espace (Paris: Presses Universitaires de France, 1957).

TR = La Terre et les rêverie du repos: Essai sur les images de l'intimité (Paris: José Corti, 1948).

TV = La Terre et les rêveries de la volonté: Essai sur l'imagination des forces (Paris: José Corti, 1948).

TRANSLATIONS

The Psychoanalysis of Fire, trans. by A.C.M. Ross (Boston: Beacon Press, 1968).

The Philosophy of No: A Philosophy of the New Scientific Mind, trans. G.C. Waterston (New York: Orion Press, 1969).

The Poetics of Reverie: Childhood, Language, and the Cosmos, trans. D. Russell (Boston: Beacon Press, 1971).

The Poetics of Space, trans. M. Jolas (Boston: Beacon Press, 1994).

Air and Dreams: An Essay on the Imagination of Movement, trans. E.R. and C.F. Farrell (Dallas: Dallas Institute Publications, 2002).

Water and Dreams: An Essay on the Imagination of Matter, trans. E.R. Farrell (Dallas: Dallas Institute Publications, 1983).

Lautréamont, trans. R.S. Dupree (Dallas: Dallas Institute Publications, 1986).

A complete list of The Bachelard Translations, published by The Dallas Institute of Humanities and Culture, can be found at www.dallasinstitute.org/books_thebachelardtranslations.html.

PREFACE

By the time of his death in 1962, Gaston Bachelard had not only written twenty-three widely acclaimed books. He had established an extraordinary reputation throughout France as an influential and iconoclastic professor who spoke of intellectual revolutions from within the sanctuary of the very traditional Sorbonne. For his students, his last years at the university were a period of enchanted discovery, as they profited also from the rich commentaries provided by his colleagues and disciples (Georges Canguilhem, Jean Hyppolite)." [1] During the past two decades, however, Bachelard's name has been almost totally absent from philosophical debate. To be sure, his notion of "rupture epistemologique" has been widely adopted by philosophers, physicists, biologists, and sociologists, including Louis Althusser, Michel Foucault, and Pierre Bourdieu. Yet a book such as *Le Même et l'autre: quarante-cinq ans de philosophie française* (1979), whose title, at least, gives the impression of a certain inclusiveness, barely mentions his name." [2] Its author, Vincent Descombes, chooses instead to focus on the most visible or the "most talked about" philos-

---

1 They were both influential university professors. Canguilhem, an epistemologist, was to follow Bachelard at the head of the Institut d'Histoire des Sciences at the University of Paris. He repeatedly acknowledged his debt to Bachelard. See his *La Connaissance de la vie* (Paris: Hachette, 1952) and *Études d'histoire et de philosophie des sciences* (Paris: Vrin, 1968). Hyppolite, a historian of philosophy and specialist of Hegel, lectured on Bachelard. They both participated in the volume *Hommage à Gaston Bachelard* (Paris: Presses Universitaires de France, 1957).
2 Vincent Descombes, *Le Même et l'autre: quarante-cinq ans de philosophie française* (Paris: Éditions de Minuit, 1979).

ophy, born from the rereading of "the masters of suspicion": Marx, Nietzsche, and Freud. It is true that Bachelard does not have an obvious place in this debate. As Mary McAllaster suggests in "Bachelard Twenty Years On," his humanism, albeit a subversive one, marked his philosophy as "outdated when humanism became," as she says, "inadmissible." [3]

Bachelard obsolete? Far from it. The contentious and at times deafening polemics of the philosophical avant-garde have not totally muted his voice. His work is an important reference for many influential thinkers of our times who could not, however, be called his disciples. A rigorous structuralist like Michel Serres, for instance, declared in the first volume of *Hermes* (1969): "Once more, we have to start from Bachelard." [4] That is, we need to meditate upon the lesson of his dual attempt to define a new scientific mind and a new criticism. Serres sees Bachelard as both "the last of the Symbolists" and a prophetic thinker. He states that, by its very open-endedness, Bachelard's dual pursuit designates the essential philosophical moment from which the destinies of science and of cultural analysis (understood as the study of myth) must be perceived as inseparable, even though they each pursue their own non-Bachelardian course.

The rapprochement between philosophy and literature has been a dominant characteristic of continental thought since World War II. Bachelard's crucial contribution to this orientation, however, is quite different from the existentialists' inclusion of the *vécu* (the lived experience) within philosophical reflection. By questioning the nature and the formation of scientific concepts, Bachelard forces philosophy to analyze the mythology that either contaminates, accompanies, or supports the progression of thought toward truth. In "La mythologie blanche," Jacques Derrida identifies Bachelard as a point of departure in this project, as offering a new reflection on the necessary link between the language of philosophy and metaphoric language. [5]

3   Mary McAllaster, "Bachelard Twenty Years On," *Revue de Littérature Comparée* 58, no. 2 (1984): 165–76.
4   Michel Serres, *La Communication*, 2nd ed. (Paris: Éditions de Minuit, 1984), p. 21.
5   In Jacques Derrida, *Marges de la philosophie* (Paris: Éditions de Minuit, 1972),

Starting from an epistemological concern, Bachelard has contributed
to what Derrida calls "cracking the surface of philosophy" by focus-
ing on the dispersion of meaning through metaphors.

There are other signs indicating that a new Bachelardian criticism has emerged from within contemporary philosophy. A few
young philosophers have challenged specific aspects of Bachelard's
work: Dominique Lecourt and Michel Vadée from the point of view
of historical materialism; Jean-Pierre Roy in the name of the "scien-
tificité" of modern literary criticism. [6] Their books, however parti-
san, are healthy attempts to break both the spell cast by Bachelard
upon his admirers and the relative silence surrounding his work.
Nothing would have pleased Bachelard more than to have become
the animator of this continuing philosophical polemic.

On this side of the Atlantic, Bachelard's legacy has suffered greatly from the capricious dynamics of our modern intellectual Babel,
although he is certainly not its only victim. Try as we might to up-
hold the myth of dialogue through symposia and colloquia, trans-
cultural communications remain subject to intellectual fashions,
mutual incomprehension, and above all to the haphazard pace of
translations. When, in the mid-sixties, I approached several university presses with my project of selected translations from the works
of Gaston Bachelard, the initial response was invariably "Gaston
who?" Editors were either totally unaware of his work, or they were
trying to figure out whether this philosopher, who dabbled in criticism, was a pataphysician or some kind of structuralist. Then, in
1970, as this book entered the final stages of a long editing process,
a survey of the academic market conducted by its publisher conclud-
ed that Bachelard was pretty much "over the hill" as far as contemporary literary criticism was concerned. The enormous fascination
of structuralism had by then eclipsed the thematic and phenomeno-

---

pp. 247–324. English trans. by F.C.T. Moore: "White Mythology," New Literary
History 6, no. 1 (1974): 5–74.
6   Dominique Lecourt, Bachelard: Le Jour et la nuit (Paris: Grasser, 1974); Michel
Vadée, Bachelard ou le nouvel idéalisme épistemologique (Paris: Éditions Sociales,
1975); Jean-Pierre Roy, Bachelard ou le concept contre l'image (Montreal: Presses
Universitaires de Montréal, 1977).

logical approaches to literature with which Bachelard was associated. By the time he had begun to become known in this country, his
work was already considered "dépassé."

This short anthology, whose goal was to offer an English reading
public a sampling of Bachelard's meditations on the poetic image,
was therefore out of "synchronicity" (to borrow the Jungian term)
with the development of critical theories. A certain temporal logic
would seem to dictate that what was already out of date in 1970 is
even more so today. On the contrary, I believe now is the time to reread Bachelard with the benefit of distance and of the renewed critical pluralism of our times.

Bachelard's books were not available in English until 1964 when
The Psychoanalysis of Fire (1938) and *The Poetics of Space* (1957) appeared.
They represent, respectively, the first and one of the last volumes,
among many, that Bachelard devoted specifically to the study of the
imagination. In 1969, *The Poetics of Reverie* (1960) and *The Philosophy
of No* (1940) were published. Strangely, *The Right to Dream* (1971), a
posthumous collection of essays, almost immediately followed the
publication of the French original. But more than forty years separate *Lautréamont* (1939) and *L'Eau et les rêves* (1942) from their English
versions (*Water and Dreams*, 1983; *Lautréamont*, 1986).

Literary criticism is not the only field in which the author has been
more or less ignored. The lack of communication is even more striking in the domain of the philosophy of science. In his "Introduction
to the English Edition" of *Marxism and Epistemology: Bachelard,
Canguilhem, Foucault* (London: NLB, 1975), Dominique Lecourt discusses "the riddle of the protracted mutual ignorance" that has
prevented a dialogue between the parallel works of Karl Popper in
Austria and Gaston Bachelard in France. A similar phenomenon
separates the works of Thomas Kuhn and Bachelard. While Kuhn's
The Structure of Scientific Revolutions was translated into French in 1972,
Bachelard's epistemological work remains practically unknown in
the United States. *Le Nouvel esprit scientifique* (1934), already part of
the French university curriculum in the 1940s, was destined to wait
half a century before appearing in English. Only continental critics,
Lecourt remarked in 1975, "have thought that they could detect an

accord between Kuhn's theses and the Bachelardian epistemological current." But such comparative epistemology is still very superficial, as Lecourt aptly demonstrates.

One limitation of the present selection, as I now see it, is the absence of texts from the epistemological works. Although I believed at the time of its conception, as I do now, that it is essential to study Bachelard's philosophy of science in order to understand the philosophical thrust of his works on the imagination, I thought that a brief presentation of his epistemology with my introduction would be sufficient. I would be more leery today of the dangers of disassociating these two sides of his work. I envisage many possible additions to this anthology. Selections illustrating the radical break between immediate and scientific knowledge, showing why a "false science" never *becomes* true, would be central. The vivid pages on the "rupture" between alchemy and chemistry, or between the first atomistic intuitions and quantum physics, in particular, come to mind. I would also include texts on the cultural and subjective significance of the most extravagant prescientific explanations. Such passages abound in *La Formation de l'esprit scientifique*, a book Jean Starobinski referred to as "a poetics of error" and Michel Serres called a "treatise on sottise." [7] Going to the other end of the scientific spectrum, I would add descriptions of those peculiar reveries and aesthetic emotions evoked by pure mathematical forms. In sum, I would delineate more clearly the boundaries between Bachelard's epistemology and his poetics, and at the same time emphasize the problematic nature of these boundaries.

In the absence of translations, there exist now several good English presentations of Bachelard's epistemology. Mary Tiles's *Bachelard: Science and Objectivity* is a fine study of Bachelard's epistemology and its relation to the "gulf" that exists between "continental" thought and Anglo-Saxon analytical philosophy. [8] Roch Smith's

---

7   Jean Starobinski, "La double légitimité," *Revue Internationale de Philosophie* 150 (1984): 232; Michel Serre, "La réforme et les sept péchés," *L'Arc* 42 (1970): 14.
8   Mary Tiles, *Bachelard: Science and Objectivity* (Cambridge: Cambridge University Press, 1984).

Bachelard is an excellent introduction to Bachelard's entire œuvre.[9] It is a sensitive and scrupulous intellectual biography that follows Bachelard's development from La Valeur inductive de la relativité (1929) to La Flamme d'une chandelle (1961). Smith is very attentive to the actual rhythm of Bachelard's writing, to its moments of rupture and to the cross-fertilization between scientific and poetic cultures. He ultimately finds in epistemology the source of Bachelard's unity:

> The real question is why, despite Bachelard's demonstrated ability to treat topics from a rigorously conceptual approach – one whose affinities with structuralism have been pointed out – he chooses a different means when it comes to literature. The answer is to be found in his recognition of the essential uniqueness of imaginative literature ... Such a recognition leads to an approach that Bachelard himself labeled "hermeneutic," ... an approach that is consistent with his fundamental position that philosophy must learn from the object of its analysis and with the related view that error stems from the imposition of a priori categories (p. 137).

The question of the unity and/or duality of Bachelard's philosophy remains a major preoccupation of his commentators. One need only scan the titles of the numerous studies on Bachelard to be convinced of the importance and the difficulty of this question: "Sur une épistémologie concordataire"; "Gaston Bachelard ou le romantisme de l'intelligence"; "Unité de pensée chez Bachelard: Valeurs et langage"; "La double legitimité"; "Janus Bifrons"; "Bachelard: Le four et la nuit."[10] Indeed, one cannot avoid presenting Bachelard as an author working in two disciplines, or rather in two areas of culture, whose study requires diametrically opposed approaches. To the relentless repression, by the scientific mind of its own subjectivity, he opposes the adventurous openness and receptivity of the dreaming

9   Roch Smith, Bachelard (Boston: Twayne Publishers, 1982).
10   In order of their listing, these studies are by Georges Canguilhem and Jean Hyppolite in Hommage, pp. 3–12 and 13–27; Mary McAllaster in Bachelard: Colloque de Cerisy (Paris: Union Generate d'Éditions, 1974), pp. 91–110; Jean Starobinski and Gilles Gaston Granger in Revue Internationale de Philosophie 150, no. 3: 231–44 and 257–71; and Dominique Lecourt, Bachelard.

cogito. To the notion that science can be analyzed conceptually, he contrasts the conviction that the study of poetry requires imagination and sympathy. Does it follow that Bachelard is *un penseur double*? If so, should this duality be questioned or accepted?

To complicate matters further, the question of whether Bachelard's thought is a cohesive unity goes beyond the presence in his work of two separate realms of investigation, the scientific and the poetic. It also emerges from the plurality of methods and philosophies that Bachelard summons in each of his enterprises. His epistemology strives to formulate in philosophical terms the convergence (Canguilhem's "concordat") between reason and experience actively demonstrated by modern science. In his studies on poetic imagination, the plurality of critical approaches can become quite disconcerting. Indeed, this plurality is not fairly represented by saying that he successively uses a psychoanalytical and a phenomenological approach, the latter being much more congenial to his quest for what Georges Poulet has termed the "indetermination" of a subjectivity without form. [11] Furthermore, his philosophical position seems difficult to define, since he is excruciatingly demanding and distrustful of philosophy in his epistemological work, while he philosophizes with the greatest abandon in his poetics.

For many commentators, the duality serves mainly as an impetus to search for an underlying unity, be it philosophical, logical, or psychological. The most deceptively reassuring approach in this direction consists in describing the evolution of the author, exploiting the multiple "confessions" interspersed throughout his works of his oscillation between his two interests. This evolutionary view is generally adopted by critics who valorize imaginary life. In its extreme form, it focuses on a phase of resolution, by the imagination, of the residual questions left open by scientific knowledge. Jacques Gagey, for instance, founds his analysis on the notion of "conversion" to the imagination (a notion adopted by many other critics). [12] He shows

11 Georges Poulet, "Bachelard et l'indétermination," *Revue de Littérature Comparée* 58, no. 2 (1984): 137–43.
12 Jacques Gagey, *Gaston Bachelard ou la conversion à l'imaginaire* (Paris: Marcel Rivière, 1969).

Bachelard progressively yielding to the forces of "the imaginary" and
enjoying in poetry the reconciliation with himself and the world that
science does not allow. It is not that such a description is entirely
false but that it is dangerously reductive. It substitutes a comforting
psychological fiction of continuity for a study of the refined dialectics that Bachelard ceaselessly pursued both in his poetics and in his
epistemology. The assumption underlying this abusive privileging of
the imagination is that the world must be understood as one. This
assumption should not be confused, however, with Jean Hyppolite's
suggestive hypothesis that Bachelard's "two thematics are developed
out of a single thought, a single imaginative project, which is a project of total opening [ouverture intégrale]." [13]

The "theory" of a conversion to the forces of subjectivity is quite
pervasive among critics, and it may be partly responsible for the
strong reaction against "Bachelardism" by some proponents of "scientific" literary criticism. Jean-Pierre Roy provides an example of
this reaction in his study Bachelard ou le concept contre l'image. For Roy,
Bachelard's duality of methods is simply unacceptable. The assertion that images cannot be studied conceptually but must be "lived"
or even "relived" serves only to mask, as Roy sees it, a "humanist
ideology" of literature and its accompanying belief in hermeneutics.
He criticizes Bachelard, in other words, for holding to the notion of
a universal human nature or subject conceived as the source of interpretation. "Bachelard's literary reflection recaptures the ontology
banned from his epistemology, and in particular a cogito excluded
from an explicitly non-Cartesian epistemology" (p. 217).

While this well-documented book is certainly of interest for the
way in which it shows Bachelard on the verge of fully recognizing
that the inventiveness of literature stems from the productivity of
language rather than from a pre-existing subjective meaning, Roy's
analysis of Bachelard serves to support his own systematic rejection
of all types of hermeneutic criticism, whether they have preceded or
ignored the advent of scientific linguistics. In sum, Roy disqualifies

13   Jean Hyppolite, "Gaston Bachelard ou le romantisme de l'intelligence," in
Hommage, p. 25.

Bachelard's poetics for doing what Gagey finds most worthwhile in it, namely, restoring a philosophy of values based on a philosophy of the subject.

A comparable difference of opinion was illustrated at the 1968 colloquium on *Les Chemins actuels de la critique*. While Hélène Tuzet showed the rejuvenating influence of Bachelard on literary criticism, Jean Ricardou expressed his misgivings, and those of the *Tel Quel* group, concerning both the importance and the validity of Bachelard's "frivolous" reading of Poe. Interestingly, one of Bachelard's defenders in the ensuing discussion was Gerard Genette, who certainly could not be suspected of promoting a subjective criticism. Genette admired in Bachelard "what Borges calls an ecumenical sensibility for literature" [14] and indicated the need for a parallel openness in criticism.

Bachelard, then, has been caught in the middle of an ideological confrontation between "the old new criticism" and "the new new criticism," as Todorov characterized the two main tendencies of the sixties. In this debate, he has been made accountable for a critical project that was not necessarily his own but that of his followers, however diverse they have been. Exploiting Bachelard's books in piecemeal fashion, some eager theoreticians and imitators have extracted from them the most easily transposable models for a typology of images. Others have overlooked the labyrinthine construction of Bachelard's reveries to find in his flights of associations an inspiration for psychological ramblings. [15] But his best readers have always been lucid about these dangers and have defined their own methods independently from the benefit they drew from Bachelard's insights. Poulet sums up this attitude very well: "This criticism, whose only goal is to find the poetic essence of all existences, is perfectly capable of finding *poetry* but incapable of distinguishing *different kinds*

14   Hélène Tuzet, "Les voies ouvertes par Gaston Bachelard à la critique," *Les Chemins actuels de la critique* (Paris: Union Generale d'Éditions: 1968), pp. 300–12; Jean Ricardou, "Un étrange lecteur," ibid., pp. 312–20. Genette's remark appears in the "discussion" following these two papers, p. 328.

15   Robert Champigny rightly points out the danger of a possible cooptation of Bachelard by superficial forms of psychological thematism. See "Gaston Bachelard," in *Modern French Criticism*, ed. John K. Simon (Chicago: University of Chicago Press, 1972), pp. 175–91.

of poetry." [16] The English comparatist John G. Clark demonstrates how Bachelard, in spite of his use of truncated and sometimes poorly translated quotations, succeeded in opening new perspectives in the reading of Shelley and other British authors. For both Poulet and Clark, the unique, exemplary value of Bachelard lies in his ability to let a text astonish and provoke, to remain constantly in contact with what Clark calls "the live mystery" of the poem ("le vif mystérieux du texte") while creating multiple intertextual correspondences with other authors. [17]

The work of Bachelard stands beyond the disputes of critical theory as a monumental reflection on human knowledge and creativity. If I believe that a return to Bachelard is important at this moment in the history of Western thought, it is not in the hope of reviving a parochial Bachelardian criticism but of seeing Bachelard take his proper place in the current philosophical debate on human culture and its interpretation. The dual direction of his inquiry should remain for us a provocative focus of interrogation, as it was for him.

Bachelard often defined the vocation of philosophy in very traditional and humanistic terms, as in this statement from one of his courses: "The dramatic problem of philosophy is how to integrate scientific truths within human reality." His life's work, however, was not devoted to formulating a solution to this problem, despite his numerous allusions to his progress toward a personal equilibrium. His philosophy strives, on the contrary, to further dramatize the challenge posed to philosophical thinking by the co-existence of our humanist and scientific cultures. This challenge can be rephrased in more contemporary terms: is it possible to reconcile the quest for truth and the quest for meaning? The first is guided by an increasingly abstract mathematical formalism; the second deals with the

16   Georges Poulet, "Bachelard et la critique contemporaine," in *Currents of Thought in French Literature: Essays in Memory of G.T. Clapton* (New York: Barnes and Noble, 1966), p. 357.
17   John G. Clark, "Cinq images de Shelley qui ont fasciné Bachelard," *Revue Internationale de Philosophie* 150 (1984): 289.

symbols carried by our common, ancestral language, which is loaded with significations adverse to formalization. On the side of truth,
real progress toward objectivity is measured by successive scientific
revolutions; on the side of meaning, it seems that culture only repeats itself through variations on the symbolic content of our myths.
What language then can the philosopher use? [18] Bachelard's critical examination of philosophy stems from his conviction that traditional philosophies have exhausted their power to renew their own
language because of their ambition to define on their own the life of
the mind. Instead of trying to improve on the contents of previous
systems, he ceaselessly questions the role of philosophy in relation
to the other productions of the human mind.

This attitude is clear in Bachelard's reflection on the nature of scientific thought and in his critique of the philosophy of science. He
salutes in passing the perennial reflexive orientation of philosophy:
"One is not a philosopher if one does not become aware, at one point
or another, of the coherence and unity of the mind" (PN: 3). But he
castigates philosophy for "boasting about its cloture," for legislat-
ing the nature of knowledge without accepting the lessons of science
("se mettre a l'école de la science"). The "philosopher" who becomes
the butt of Bachelard's criticism and irony believes that reason is im-
mutable, or that the electron is a speck of matter, or that experience
and intuition are the same thing. In any case, he embodies the capital
sin of philosophy: the pretension to define the nature of reason while
disregarding the actual functioning of scientific thought. Bachelard
traces the source of this philosophical hubris to the Cartesian cogito.
"The identity of the mind in the I think is so clear that the science of

18 "The philosopher who meditates on today's problems of scientific thought
is at a crossroads: should his reflection lead to an integration of the sciences
within a renovated philosophy or to an integration of philosophy within an
elaborate scientific thought? ... But he has barely made his choice when he receives the most contradictory advice: be precise, says the technician, no superfluous details, says the philosopher, be exact and rigorous, says the mathema-
tician, ... tell us to what philosophical school we must refer the philosophy of
contemporary science, says the historian of philosophy, without considering
that scientists are, strangely and symptomatically, scrupulous in avoiding any
metaphysical affirmation." "Introduction" to Bachelard's L'Activité rationaliste
de la physique contemporaine, pp. 5–6.

that clear consciousness is immediately the consciousness of a science, the certainty of founding a philosophy of knowledge" (PN: 9). This passage contains a sketch of a deconstructive orientation of philosophy. In stressing the obligation for a philosophy of knowledge to explore the "formation," if not the genealogy, of its own concepts, to learn what is objectivity not from the concept of science but from science being done *now*, Bachelard signals a profound transformation of the concept of philosophy.

Bachelard does not fully pursue this line of thought. The systems displaced from their royal position are replaced, in his epistemology, by the figure of an absent philosophy, yet to come, which will eventually be in harmony with its contemporary science. Dominique Lecourt has cogently analyzed the paradoxical character of this epistemology in his *Bachelard: Le Jour et la nuit*. Bachelard indeed reiterates, from book to book and with an array of future and conditional tenses, his call for a new philosophy of the sciences, as if to suggest his own work did not constitute a realization of this project. Even more paradoxically, he condemns past philosophies for not being adequate to science while at the same time retaining their ideal of a correspondence between philosophy and science. Lecourt solves this philosophical puzzle by tracking down a hidden contradiction between Bachelard's intention to build a materialist philosophy and the unconscious idealism inherent in his belief in the possibility of a philosophy of science. In addition, says Lecourt, Bachelard "re-centers" in his poetics a philosophy of idealist values because his epistemology has not been able to solve this contradiction.

For all his elegant and original investigation, Lecourt may not entirely convince his readers that Bachelard's project was essentially materialist or that any "materialist epistemology" is a theoretical monstrosity alongside the "only coherent" materialism, historical materialism. If we do not consider multiplicity as a monstrosity, we may find that the voyage through contradictions is more productive than the pattern of potential coherence present in or imposed upon Bachelard's work.

The conviction that "philosophy" has failed and perhaps is condemned to fail necessarily affects Bachelard's conception of "method." He used to say in his courses: "I would like to develop a philosophy that has no point of departure," adding, "a philosophy that is not a point of departure." Any discourse has nevertheless to follow a certain order. What is then the place and role of a *method* in philosophy? This was one of the questions pursued by Bachelard in his last years of teaching, a period in which he did not publish any work on the imagination. He also questioned in his courses such notions as "unity," "system," "synthesis," and their counterpart "paradox," along with the taunting points of departure "experience" and "matter." Perhaps he needed a reflective pause after his efforts to systematize material, formal, and dynamic imagination in his books on the elements.

Yet, even in his most systematic moments, Bachelard never lets his readers forget that the word *method* has a double connotation. It suggests the rigor of a system and the indeterminacy carried by its Greek root *hodos* (way); it mixes personal discovery and conceptual construction. Bachelard's methodological shifts can therefore be interpreted in terms other than "evolution" or "inconsistency." A method is both necessary and dangerous. As a way of approaching things, of initiating a discourse, it must be guided by principles, but these principles have a tendency to become frozen into a system divorced from its "formation," thereby paralyzing discovery. The dead formula of a system runs the risk of becoming "a dictatorship of the mind." "Anti-systematic philosophies," Bachelard stated in his course, "started out by being simply methods, but there is nothing more dogmatic than a philosophy of method ... In the reign of thought, imprudence is a method."

Imagination is the very support of this imprudence, while at the same time possessing its own direction and order. "Metaphors are not mere idealizations that go on like rockets, displaying their in significance by bursting in the sky" (PF: 213). If imagination is at the core of all methodological dynamism and invention, is there in turn a method capable of explaining both the production and the efficiency of images? In other words, is there a method of methods, and if so what can be its guiding concepts? This is the question raised in the conclusion of *The Psychoanalysis of Fire* and examined again in *Lautréamont*. If a poetic mind, as Bachelard has discovered it in studying images of fire, is simply a "syntax" of metaphors, "each poet, then, should give rise to a *diagram* indicating the direction and the symmetry of his metaphorical coordinations" (PF: 213). In *Lautréamont* he borrows other mathematical notions – or are they metaphors? – in order to study images in "groups," according to the laws of a "projective poetry." In both works, the search for a relevant method for his "metapoetics" does not lead outside the realm of images, but to a theoretical language that gives access to "metaphors of metaphors" (PF: 215 and L: 155).

Such passages should help reevaluate the opposition that Bachelard strategically establishes, elsewhere in his work, between concept and image. We already know that the rectified concepts of science do not cure the metaphorical impulse. Here Bachelard shows that a systematic study of metaphors restores the evocative power of certain words (such as *groups* and *diagrams*) used in other domains as concepts, and he indicates at the same time the difficulty of formulating a concept of metaphor other than by the expression "metaphor of metaphors." As Derrida has shown in "La Mythologie blanche," Bachelard's methodological attempts can be read as an illustration of the incapacity of conceptual thought to recapture its own origin. It therefore seems insufficient to characterize Bachelard's poetic methods as implying that images should be studied imaginatively since his discussion of the notion of method has broader implications concerning the discourse of philosophy.

It is also ironic that his successive poetic "methods" have been criticized for being nothing more than "intellectual metaphors" because he does not rigorously apply a model. His reappropriation of psychoanalysis is particularly interesting in this respect. Jean-François Lyotard, for instance, has noted that Bachelard's use of psychoanalysis is "of the order of word play or usurpation." [19] It is

19 Jean-François Lyotard, "L'eau prend le ciel: proposition de collage pour figurer le désir bachelardien," *L'Arc* 42: 49. My remark does not do justice to Lyotard's "proposition," a richly suggestive "collage" that grapples with the multiplicity of Bachelard's intuitions by creating a labyrinth of quotations. His attempt to trace the ramifications of Bachelard's dialectics of the feminine and

true that Bachelard never read Freud very closely and that he used the term *unconscious* as an equivalent for the metaphor of "depth" so as to disentangle imagination from the overbearing visual connotations of the word *image*. Yet his preoccupation with several key analytical notions is a constant of his work. While he condemns psychoanalysis in general for what he sees as its excessively reductive causal explanations, and while he repeatedly attacks "the psychoanalyst" in a style reminiscent of his insistent criticism of "the philosopher" found throughout his epistemological works, [20] he also sketches the figure of a "successful" psychoanalysis that would lead to a reconciliation of the individual psyche with the universe. In this respect, Michel Serres is justified in calling Bachelard the last psychoanalyst. His poetics of the cosmos delineates a generalized therapy "in which the unconscious-body is replaced by the unconscious-nature." [21]

Besides his well-known reference to Jung's theory of archetypes, Bachelard uses many other psychoanalytical sources whenever they can be useful to his own reworking of the notions of the unconscious and sublimation. He draws inspiration from Marie Bonaparte's "organic materialism" in her reading of Edgar Allan Poe and from Robert Desoille's therapy through directed dreams. In *The Poetics of Space* he finds himself in sympathy with an analysis of Michel Leiris by the contemporary psychoanalyst J.B. Pontalis who has formulated, according to Bachelard, the central truth of a "phenomenology of expression": "The speaking subject is the entire subject" (p. 11). This passage is one among many that point to a fundamental convergence of interest between Bachelard's poetics and psychoanalysis, both of which focus on the unconscious dimension of language. For Bachelard,

---

masculine throughout the problematic of method points to the need for further critical study in this direction, as well as in that of the notion of androgyny.

20 "The healthy psyche is defined as the psyche of a majority taken from a given social group, from a closed society ... Classical psychoanalysis is under the dependence of this definition of normality according to the majority." Lecture given in 1938 at the École des Hautes Études de Gand, quoted by Jean Lescure in *Un Été avec Bachelard* (Paris: Luneau Ascot, 1983), p. 54.

21 Michel Serres, *La Communication*, p. 26. On the value of Bachelard's writings for psychotherapy, see James Hillman, "Bachelard's Lautréamont, Or, Psychoanalysis without a Patient," in *Lautréamont*, trans. Robert S. Dupree (Dallas: The Dallas Institute Publications, 1986).

poetic language works, not as a revelation of past conflicts or trau-
mas but as a reconciling force that at the same time effectuates and
enlarges subjective life.

With this in mind, Bachelard's quest for a formulation of the unconscious dynamics of poetic images may be reconsidered in view
of the writings of Nicolas Abraham and Maria Torok, philosophers
and psychoanalysts whose work is also concerned with problems of
literary analysis and translation. The first part of their book L'Écorce et
le noyau poses in rigorous philosophical terms the question of a rapprochement between phenomenology and psychoanalysis and gives
rise to a new field of inquiry they call "transphenomenology." This
notion of transphenomenology and the new light it casts on the concepts of subjectivity and temporality may provide fresh insights into
Bachelard's philosophy of imagination. [22]

When Bachelard calls on the archetypal classification of material
elements to establish a typology of images, and on psychoanalysis
and later phenomenology to explain the subjective power of the
poetic image, should we then speak of "methods"? The now familiar term of "strategy" might be more appropriate because it has
some of the experimental and even playful connotations present in
Bachelard's "methodological" shifts and reassessments. It is also
close to the notion of work (which translates travail, œuvre, and ou-
vrage), essential for Bachelard's understanding of how thought proceeds. It is the metaphor of "work" that helps him introduce a phenomenological motif in his studies long before he asserts his prefer-
ence for phenomenology over psychoanalysis. "Work" can be seen as
the Bachelardian transformation of the notion of intentionality. This
metaphor, prominent in the "ontology of struggle" he sketches in La
Terre et les rêveries de la volonté, occupies a central place, throughout his
books, in his description of the simultaneous emergence of subject
and object. When he uses Nietzsche's phrase "Thus my dream found
the world" (AS: 163), it is with the understanding that the dreamer is

---

22 Nicolas Abraham and Maria Torok, L'Écorce et le noyau (Paris: Aubier-Flam-
marion, 1978), particularly "Le symbole ou l'au-delà du phenomene," pp. 25–
76. For further reading, see "Psychoanalytic Esthetics: Time, Rhythm, and the
Unconscious," Diacritics (Fall 1986): 3–14.

never passive. Not only is the imagination at work on imaginary matter, but the scientific *no* is also at work *against* a kind of matter, the fixed language of theory. Scientists are "laborers" ("travailleurs de la preuve") striving to "de-realize" and "transplant" scientific notions.

Such a generalized metaphorization of "work" can lead to the criticism that Bachelard has a blind spot toward social and historical "reality," since his description may appear as the work of a dreamer – or in Marxist vocabulary, of a "crypto-idealist" – who seeks to absorb all human struggles into an imaginary adversity. This criticism, particularly applicable to Bachelard's utopian pedagogy, is also suggested from a different perspective by Michel Serres at the end of his reading of *La Formation de l'esprit scientifique*.[23] The final chapter of this book claims indeed to present merely "the outline, drawn with a light hand, of an academic utopia" (FES: 245). For Bachelard, pedagogy is an essential category of thought and not a mere application of the general principles of knowledge to the teaching of the ignorant. Science educates itself through the continuous and collective process of error correction and is by nature in a state of constant pedagogy. The ideal scientific community ("la cité scientifique"), where teachers and students are engaged in the production of knowledge while constantly exchanging and even subverting their roles, becomes the model for any school, and "School" is in turn the ultimate model for society (FES: 252). The theme of the School, pervasive throughout his epistemological work, becomes the necessary mediation between science and philosophy or between the individual and society. The Bachelardian School does not have to confront outside forces since it effectuates, inside, the catharsis of all the elements adverse to knowledge. In this direction, the work of Michel Foucault can be seen as

---

23   "La réforme," 28. In "Reform and the Seven Sins," Serres's main critical perspective is that Bachelard's book is less a work of epistemology – even less a psychoanalytical study – than a treatise on ethics. It is not a demonstration of the "formation" of the scientific mind but a cathartic exhortation to liberate the scientific mind from attitudes in fact very close to five of the capital sins (avarice, sloth, gluttony, lust, and pride), the two others (envy and wrath) acting as virtues in the scientific enterprise.

completing and correcting Bachelard, albeit implicitly, by analyzing the effects of power on and within knowledge. [24]

There is a still largely unexplored dimension in the persistent play of reversibility Bachelard establishes between two terms linked by a preposition, as in "metaphor *of* work." We are authorized by his descriptions and analyses to read "metaphor *as* work," as the power of language to promote being. Similarly, "phenomenology of the image" becomes "image as phenomenology." This is perhaps why Bachelard, in his choice of rhetorical terms, ultimately favors "correspondence" over "metaphor." The latter perpetuates to some extent the illusion that there might be, somewhere in the world, a proper meaning that predates the image. In a correspondence, on the contrary, the two words "exchange their powers" and supplement rather than supplant each other. Thus Bachelard seeks a new theoretical language by reappropriating rhetorical notions, just as he does previous theories, so as to disrupt the traditional hierarchy between concept and image. The word he borrows has to be marked by a coefficient of dynamism that precludes the possibility of assigning a fixed point of departure to the image or the concept. Sometimes it is a doubling, as in "metaphor of metaphor"; sometimes it is a prefix, like *sur* or *meta*, as in surrationalism and metapsychology. [25] It seems that, for him, no theoretical language escapes the metaphoric displacement.

My re-reading of Bachelard has led me to resist or at least to qualify the widely accepted interpretation that his poetics represents the completion of his philosophy while his epistemology is imbued with a profound distrust of philosophy. Because he audaciously announces a "metaphysics of the imagination" in his first non-epistemological books and because the "micrometaphysical study" of reverie, which

24 Particularly in *L'Ordre du discours* (Paris: Gallimard, 1971). On deconstruction as a struggle to transform education, see Jacques Derrida, "Où commence et comment finit un corps enseignant," in *Politiques de la philosophie*, ed. Dominique Grisoni (Paris: Grasser, 1976).

25 See Gabriel Germain, "L'imagination poétique et la notion de métapsychologie," in *Bachelard: Colloque de Cerisy*, pp. 182–95.

he pursues in the following works, reveals the emergence and modifications of *being* through imaginary life, it may seem legitimate to read the outline of an ontology in this part of his work. But Bachelard's "philosophy" of imagination never addresses the question "what is being?" It focuses instead on the linguistic experiences that reveal, in *being*, an irresistible movement toward well-being. His work is unified by the desire to demonstrate the integrating force of imagination, and it evolves into a cosmotherapy rather than an ontology. To be sure, imaginary life is not random; its description is organized on the basis of a system of symbols that Bachelard adopted partly from the pre-Socratics, partly from the Romantics. But when he confronts the question of the source of poetic language, he opts for indetermination. The more reverie expands to the dimensions of the cosmos, the more the limits between the world and the subject become blurred. Many passages tend to place the world in the position of the speaking subject. Bachelard resists the attraction of a Romantic metaphysics that would turn the imagining subject into a mouthpiece for a transcendent being. As a result, we are left with the unresolved question "who speaks, the dreamer or the world?" (PR: 161). It is not surprising that, in *La Communication*, Michel Serres praises Bachelard for making possible a new chapter in the study of our cultural myths. Because Bachelard exhausted the possibilities of extending the domain of a symbolist analysis, the true legacy of his dual pursuit might appear, according to Serres, in the direction of a new *logo-analysis* that will apply refined structural methods to cultural elements.

Furthermore, the subject that Bachelard reintroduces in his description of the poetic experience is deprived of the deductive and constitutive powers of the Cartesian *cogito*. It is a subject that can only discover and rediscover itself in the poetic instant as a "minimum of being" (PR: 95). This rarefied *cogito* breathes at the center of a solitary wisdom bordering on mysticism; it is not, for Bachelard, the foundation of a metaphysics. It suggests instead a philosophical direction quite different from his poetics of archetypes, which could be called a poetics or an ethics of solitude.

It is perhaps the ethical dimension of Bachelard's work on the imagination that explains the view, expounded by several of his commentators, that his philosophy gravitates around a unifying axiology. In all his works, but particularly in his poetic texts, values are indeed clearly polarized. The "good" appears to depend on a healthy dialectics between the "real" and the "unreal." Paraphrasing Bachelard, we could say that a true image – an image really imagined – is also an image that contains a truth about human reality. Such an image, by expanding the subject, is necessarily a source of happiness. Bachelard, however, does not develop a full-fledged philosophy of values. His books offer lessons for working, reading, breathing, and dreaming well, all of which constitute an art of living poetically. Bachelard's lyrical confidence in the powers of imagination may lead some of his readers to accuse him of excessive optimism. His message appears indeed to be that there are no dark forces, in the individual or in humanity, that could not be happily sublimated through a full imaginary life. But his ethics point in fact toward asceticism. Throughout his work he developed the paradox that the primitiveness of poetic consciousness is not immediately given. It can only be a conquest. The Bachelardian reverie, far from being a complacent drifting of the self, is a discipline acquired through long hours of reading and writing, and through a constant practice of "surveillance de soi." Images reveal nothing to the lazy dreamer. [26]

The two parts of Bachelard's work – his epistemology and his poetics – each one following a progression dictated by its own object, display the conviction that the destiny of philosophy is to remain somehow "pluralist" or incomplete. This incompleteness is made obvious in his poetics by the tension between the meditation of the solitary dreamer and the work of the thinker in a community. For the former, sitting at his table lit by a simple candle, it seems that all metaphors become the equivalent of the flame-life he is contemplating. For the thinker in the world, the one who teaches, reads poets,

---

26   Pierre Quillet provides an excellent analysis of what he calls Bachelard's "epicurean asceticism" in his *Bachelard* (Paris: Seghers, 1964), pp. 148ff. This book is the most suggestive and complete presentation in French of Bachelard's entire corpus.

and writes books, the task is to show us how to read the complex syntax of symbols. Are metaphors destined to be subsumed under a single image, or are they defined by their power of differentiation? It seems that the question remains open and that Bachelard's "meta-poetics" is not more unified than his metaphysics.

One must recognize therefore that Bachelard has realized his project of a "dispersed" philosophy. For him, philosophy must not only turn toward other disciplines – which it has always done when in need of renewing itself. It must constantly operate on its very edge, at the very limit where its systematizing impulse is challenged by the actual creations in other domains of human activity. This is the core of the paradoxes explored and illustrated by Bachelard. In this per-spective, he appears as a "penseur-charnière" (as a hinge), not so much between the scientific and the poetic cultures as between two moments or styles of philosophy, the style of totalizing metaphysical systems and the "polyphilosophy" for which he always aimed.

C.G.
Dartmouth College
Summer 1986

INTRODUCTION

To Dream Well

Gaston Bachelard was born in Bar-sur-Aube on June 27, 1884. He spent his childhood in Champagne and after finishing high school worked as an employee in the postal service from 1903 to 1913. He had already earned his *licence* in mathematics and was studying to become an engineer when the war broke out. In 1919, after four years of military service, he began teaching physics and chemistry in the high school of his home town, where he remained until 1930. Meanwhile he had become interested in philosophy; he began graduate work at the age of 35, acquired his *licence* in 1920, *agrégation* in 1922, and *doctorat* in 1927. His dissertations for the latter were *Essai sur la connaissance approchée* and *Étude sur l'evolution d'un problème de physique: la propagation thermique dans les solides*.

Bachelard received a post at the University of Dijon, taught there ten years, and was appointed to the chair of Philosophy of Science at the Sorbonne. In 1954 he was named professor emeritus, but he continued to publish and to lecture on a part-time basis. He was elected to the Académie des Sciences Morales et Politiques in 1955 and received the Grand Prix National des Lettres in 1961, one year before his death on October 16, 1962.

Bachelard's personal charm as a professor rivaled his reputation as one of the great minds of the Sorbonne of his day. In the lecture hall he was capable of reaching out to each listener, of capturing attention with his playfulness, geniality, and genuine concern for all those around him. Only *seeming* to ramble as he spoke, he would discover and explore the images that came to him, often stopping to give a rare word its proper interval, or to create new words that somehow always seemed to have existed before. During a discussion of Paracelsus or Copernicus, for example, he would interrupt himself to begin a meditation on cookery. He would savor a thought, repeating it in various ways, building up paradox after paradox by coupling simple, direct formulas with sinuous sentences and phrases. His references to other writers were made in a casual manner – unmindful of source citations – that might have shocked a more disciplined scholar. But the origin of this apparent disregard for erudition was a boundless enthusiasm for learning and understanding that he renewed each morning by absorbing the contents of an average of six texts on a wide range of subjects.

Proceeding in this way, Bachelard was able to include his students in the creation of his philosophy – to offer them an experience as well as an education. And outside the amphitheater he was always approachable. A white-haired patriarch, with the slow gait of a farmer at home on his native plot of ground, he would stroll along the Boulevard St. Michel talking familiarly with any student or friend. During such moments the essentially paradoxical nature of his mind coincided most perfectly with his charm: speaking in earthy accents, he tended toward ethereal thoughts; what might begin with casual references to the weather or polite inquiries concerning one's health would end with reflections on the necessity to dream well.

A Mobile Unit

Looking for unity in Bachelard's work seems a vain enterprise since his intellectual profile abounds in paradoxes: a philosopher who gently mocks philosophy; a rationalist who modestly confesses that he is merely trying to become one; a dreamer who seeks to articulate the law of images. His career, ranging from austere epistemological research to sensitive studies on poetic imagination and reverie, offers a remarkable example of duality.

Within the general evolution of contemporary thought, Bachelard's work may be viewed as a prototypical illustration of the trend toward the merging of philosophy and literature. [1] However, Bachelard never developed a metaphysics capable of unifying his reflections on science and poetry. This remark should reassure the reader who approaches his work through the books on imagination that he need not subject himself to an initiation in epistemology. Yet, in introducing Bachelard, we cannot ignore the existence of this double interest on his part. Despite his repeated insistence on the distinctive – and indeed, opposed – natures of literature and scientific thought, it is possible to draw from his epistemology certain themes that permeate his entire work and which are useful for the understanding of his literary theory. Even if we do not expect a modern philosophy to be systematic, we still cannot help seeking its underlying unity of thought. But what kind of unity?

We must always bear in mind Bachelard's vigorous warnings against the temptation to unify and reduce to identicals, which he saw as one of the most important "epistemological obstacles." Instead of immobilizing the intuition by a too rapid unification, as in prescientific theories, living thought should be dominated by its "shifting character," [2] which is an ability to shake off intellectual habits, to accept the lessons of an evolving science. For Bachelard this is the *sine qua non* of the modern educator. He rejects the role of the scholar who shares the fruit of his learning in the form of established truths, and invites us to experience with him "the essential mobility of concepts." [3]

1   Existentialist writers offer the best illustration of this trend. See the commentary on the work of Simone de Beauvoir by Maurice Merleau-Ponty, "Metaphysics and the Novel," in *Sense and Nonsense*, trans. Hubert L. Drewfus and Patricia Allen Drewfus (Evanston: Northwestern University Press, 1992), pp. 26–40.

2   Bachelard borrows this expression from Alfred Korzybski, *Science and Sanity: An Introduction to Non-Aristotelian Systems and General Semantics* (New York: The International Non-Aristotelian Library Company, 1933). He devotes a passage in *La Philosophie du non* (pp. 127–34) to a commentary on the book, which he considers "a great work."

3   This is a central notion in Bachelard's philosophy. It designates not a superficial mobility that replaces one concept with another but an internal dialectic that does not need to change denominations. Modern science has progressively "rectified" ancient concepts, such as that of the atom, by detaching them from a fixed content. This mobility is equally essential to imagination.

The preservation of this *shifting character* not only is a methodological requirement; it also has a philosophical parallel in Bachelard's view of human time, which is extremely important to the understanding of his poetics. In *La Dialectique de la durée* he writes that he accepts almost everything from Bergson except the idea of continuity. [4] If time is creative, it is not by virtue of a vital permanence of the past but through a *decision* in the etymological sense of the word: the end of each instant at once signifies a new beginning. [5]

We can find another such parallel in Bachelard's conception of the discontinuity of human cultural progress – historical or individual. It is impossible to explain one stage of development, either ancient or modern, by what preceded it. A mutative pattern, rather than an additive or deductive one, expresses true progress best. In the light of this conception of time we can better appreciate Bachelard's startling statement in one of his lectures: "I should like to develop a philosophy that would have no point of departure." We must therefore be aware of the essentially rhythmic character of Bachelard's research. The general rhythm is indicated by the alternation of science and poetry in his career: they correspond to two dimensions of the psyche, *animus* and *anima*; they achieve two different potentials of human speech, and all that the philosopher can do is to enjoy both poles of his "double nature, fully recognized." On the methodological level, the same dual rhythm is found in the balance between the irony of polemics and the sympathy of enthusiasm. Contradictions and paradoxes refine concepts; they exercise the mobility of thought. A rapid outline of Bachelard's work might take the form of a list of affirmations emending one another almost

---

Reverie shatters frozen meanings and restores to old words ambivalence and freedom.

4   Georges Canguilhem notes with a certain irony: "This profession of faith seems more sincere to me in what it rejects than in what it keeps." "Sur une épistémologie concordataire," in *Hommage à Gaston Bachelard* (Paris: Presses Universitaires de France, 1957), p. 4. Indeed, Bachelard's reaction against Bergson is a profound one.

5   As Bachelard says, in lapidary fashion, "Moments differ because of their fecundity." *L'Intuition de l'instant: Étude sur la Siloë de Gaston Roupnel* (Paris: Librairie Stock, 1932), p. 86.

to the point of contradiction. Unity appears then as an *asymptotic* goal. We never possess it, we only discover in ourselves a possibility for reconciliation

It is significant that Bachelard's last work, *La Flamme d'une chandelle*, which he designated as "a little book of simple reverie," offers a convergence of his most personal themes. Reverie reconciles the world and the subject, present and past, solitude and communication. There is only one requirement: that it seek written expression, whether through original creation or through an encounter with an already existing poem. This important distinction makes Bachelard not only a spiritual master but also a philosopher who opens broader perspectives on literary criticism. [6]

The Rehabilitation of the Imagination

Bachelard is not a literary critic. If he does apply a label to himself, it is that of an avid reader, an advocate of leisurely and repeated reading. He is, however, less naive than he would like to appear, for his freshness of vision is essentially the result of long discipline.

As we have already seen, there is no attempt at a unified theory of imagination in Bachelard's works on literary creation. It is not his aim to answer such ambitious questions as: What is imagination? What is an image? Rather, he would ask: *What is our comprehension of images?* [7] To state this question more precisely, we should examine how it became an important problem to Bachelard and follow it through the various stages of his study.

6   This is critic Georges Poulet's opinion in his preface to J.-P. Richard's *Littérature et sensation* (Paris: Éditions du Seuil, 1954), p. 10.
7   This is a *reflective* attitude, in the Kantian sense, comparable to modern epistemology's approach to scientific activity. For Bachelard, poetry is a specific realm of experience opened by contact with poetic works. It is in terms of this experience of the reader that he wants to study the conditions of poetic inspiration. His approach is in opposition to the philosophical outlook of American New Criticism, which is essentially Aristotelian. See Neal Oxenhandler, "Ontological Criticism in America and France," *Modern Language Review* 55 (1960).

We must go back to *La Formation de l'esprit scientifique* to appreciate the fact that Bachelard's enthusiastic rehabilitation of imagination is not lightly undertaken; there is in it a convincing force, since
it comes from a philosopher who has thoroughly explored all the
dangers that imagination holds for objective knowledge. The sub-
title of the book, "Contribution to a Psychoanalysis of Scientific
Knowledge," indicates that the function of psychoanalysis is to sever
objectivity from individual subjectivity and to denounce "the temp-
tations that distort inductions" (PF: 16). Bachelard shows that error
always comes first. Truth is a progressive conquest; and, more important, error has a positive structure. Its very resistance to correction proves that it is not a mere defect of knowledge but the expression of deep interests and instincts that have a "strange stability."
These impulses develop into aberrant images and prolix language.
"The less we know, the more we name" (PF: 157).

By nature, the subjective projections that slow down the progress of
science are similar to the impulses that produced the first pre-scientif-
ic theories; science and poetry might very well have a common source.
On the one hand, science effectuates a spontaneous *analysis* through
the extensive use of mathematics, which depersonalizes and purifies
scientific language. Like the "sorcerer's apprentice," [8] Bachelard discovers, on the other hand, that the images science must reject have an
irresistible force, and that they tempt him to further study. The imaginative impulse – our "hunger for images" – is as basic as our yearning
for objective knowledge. The "law" of the primacy of error leads him
to his psychoanalysis of the elements.

Psychoanalysis of the Elements

La Psychanalyse du feu marks a new direction in Bachelard's personal
application of Freudian and post-Freudian views. Here the function of
depth psychology is no longer to purify objectivity but to explore the
subjective structure of material images. Among the elements favored

8   A comparison made by François Dagognet, *Gaston Bachelard, sa vie, son
œuvre, avec un exposé de sa philosophie* (Paris: Presses Universitaires de France,
1965), p. 29.

by the alchemists [9] of the past (fire, air, water, and earth), the first to command Bachelard's attention is fire because it has been for so long the object of obstinate pseudo-scientific research and has always resisted conceptualization. He finds that the nature of fire is expressed no more objectively in eighteenth-century scientific treatises than in the poetic works of D'Annunzio, Chateaubriand, Novalis, and E.T.A. Hoffmann. At the level of the elemental relationship between object and subject, "dream is stronger than experiment" (PF: 46). The texts about fire tell more about ourselves than about the external world. "Fire is more likely to smolder within the soul than beneath ashes" (PF: 35). At the end of the book Bachelard has completed his conversion to imagination: "It is reverie that delineates the furthest confines of our mind" (PF: 215).

At this point in his research Bachelard insists that singularity of images is not a gratuitous fantasy, the "pastime of a fleeting moment." Rather, "metaphors evoke one another and are coordinated more than sensations, so that a poetic mind is purely and simply a syntax of metaphors" (PF: 213). This "inspired monotony" of images points to a possible structure of oneiric life oriented by material elements.

Material elements reflect our souls; more than forms, they fix the unconscious, they provide us with a sort of direct reading of our destiny. The audacious idea of psychoanalyzing elements drew immediate attention to the originality of Bachelard's research. [10] It also placed him in an ambiguous position in relation to psychoanalysis, which is why we must attempt to delineate the unconscious zone in which he is interested.

Bachelard is too often taken simply as a psychoanalytic critic. On the other hand, some psychoanalysts reproach him for not being faithful to their doctrines. We must distinguish between his use of this discipline and his criticism of it. There is genuine enthusiasm in his discovery that references to the unconscious provide a means

9   Bachelard frequently refers to alchemy. For example: La Formation de l'esprit scientifique, p. 186; TV: 242; TR: 62; PR: 65ff.
10   Notably, Sartre's initial praise in the section entitled "Quality as a Revelation of Being" in Being and Nothingness.

of correcting realistic explanations of images. This is very obvious in La Psychanalyse du feu, probably his most Freudian book.

It is noteworthy that Bachelard changed the pattern of his titles, starting with his second book on the elements: L'Eau et les rêves. From then on the word psychoanalysis is associated almost exclusively with Freudian orthodoxy and referred to in a critical, negative manner, whereas numerous positive references are made to the more or less dissident successors of Freud, and particularly to C.G. Jung. [11]

In L'Eau et les rêves Bachelard explains his refusal to account for images in terms of organic impulses by his lack of medical knowledge, alleging that this prevents him from going to the same depths as psychoanalysis. The real reason is that he wants to seize the specific originality of the symbol without reducing it to its causes. That is why he favors the Jungian concept of "archetype," which offers the advantage of including symbolism in the unconscious. Strictly speaking, an archetype is not an image. For Jung, it is psychic energy spontaneously condensing the results of organic and ancestral experiences into images; it can be designated as the paradigm of a series of images. When Bachelard uses any psychoanalytical concept, he limits his investigation to the present life of images; he disregards the historical and anthropological background of archetypes and attempts instead an "archeology of the human soul."

In particular, he prefers reverie to nocturnal dreams. The latter are capable of beautiful visions, of amazing phantasmagorias, but they are not truly experienced. It is as though another subject were dreaming within us. Identification of the self with the dream can only be achieved after the fact, when the dream is recounted. The psychoanalyst resolves the ontological mystery of the dream by seeing in it the symbols of every man. For Bachelard such a common symbolism is unable to illuminate the variations of aesthetic images; he consequently dismisses dream lore as irrelevant to the study of imagination. He prefers to concentrate on reverie, which is not, as

11   One writer quotes excerpts of a recorded conversation in which Bachelard regretted that he discovered Jung's writings too late. See C.G. Christofides, "Gaston Bachelard and the Imagination of Matter," Revue internationale de philosophie 66 (1963), pp. 486–87.

is often believed, a dispersion of consciousness, or a loss of contact with oneself and with reality.

Solitary meditation in contact with the world is "that strange reverie that is written and indeed forms itself in the act of writing" (ER: 27). It unites paradoxically the joys of evasion and the presence of a cogito, which emerges from the shadows to the surface and is "immediately attached to its object, to its image" (PR: 131). The chapter on the "Cogito du rêveur" (PR: 124ff.) attains its fullness when it is related to the numerous analyses that show how reverie gives us a cosmos. Reverie assumes the whole universe in its images; simultaneously creative and natural, its value is indissolubly aesthetic and ontological.

Therefore, Bachelard consigns the apparatus of tests, experiments, and accounts of nocturnal dreams to depth psychology and deliberately chooses to apply his psychoanalysis to literary works. "I can only know man through reading, wonderful reading, which allows me to judge man by what he writes" (ER: 14). This predilection indicates a total confidence in human emergence and growth through language. Bachelard wants to maintain his analyses at a level that he describes as a botanical *graft*. He refuses to explore the organic sources of imagination and, in particular, sexual complexes. Rather, he seeks man above the graft, where "a culture has left its traces on nature." [12] Finally, the psychoanalyst, by seeking reality beneath the fable, destroys the primacy of the image. He gives to the symbol a conceptual rigidity – he "explains the flower by the fertilizer" (PE: 12). A graft is a true human mark; thus, it is by their "cultural signs" that Bachelard identifies complexes. For him they are not pathological fixations but spontaneous orientations of the imagination educated by reading. They can be useful designations of a fusion between natural dreams and acquired traditions. Bachelard forges for them the expression "culture complexes," and names them after authors or literary heroes: Novalis, Ophelia, Swinburne, and others.

---

12   Culture and nature are inseparably fused in our immediate environment. André Malraux illustrates a similar idea in *Les Voix du silence* (Paris: N.R.F., 1951). The artist does not start by reproducing nature; he first imitates the world of art before finding his own language. "Any artist starts with pastiche," according to Malraux, p. 310.

Nevertheless, Bachelard draws attention to their double aspect: they are stultifying or stimulating. Indeed, words are given to us already charged with cultural and utilitarian habits. They tend to become a lexical code in which the sign evaporates in favor of its meaning. Symbols in particular have a cultural past that might repeatedly tend to impose an academic mythology onto poetry. Bachelard enjoys denouncing a superficial and vain mythology such as that of the swan in Leda, by Pierre Louÿs: "The beautiful white bird was like a woman, splendid and pink like light." [13] Here, images are superimposed; they do not enrich a particular emotion. It is only when they are taken up by great poets that old myths and old words regain their significance. [14] They must in some way be reactivated by that material imagination that gives life to the elementary *correspondence* between humankind and the world. For Bachelard, imagination must infuse a second life into familiar images, it must create "metaphors of metaphors."

The Reverberation of Images

Bachelard increases his attack on psychoanalysis in his last three books. In the introduction to La Poétique de l'espace he describes an important turning point in his study of poetry. Retrospectively, he detects in the latter part of his work a persistent rationalistic "stiffness," one which he now seeks definitely to abandon for a fuller use of *phenomenology.* [15]

In a word, the phenomenological approach is a description of the immediate relationship of phenomena with a particular conscious-

13   Pierre Louÿs, Leda, ou la Louange des bienheureuses ténèbres (Paris: Librairie de l'art independant, 1893), p. 11
14   To Bachelard's innumerable examples might be added T.S. Eliot's use of myths and literary quotations in The Waste Land.
15   From phenomenology Bachelard retains above all the admonition to return to "phenomena themselves." This requires putting aside naive belief in the reality of things and approaching phenomena through consciousness that is always "intentional" – always consciousness of something. For a parallel between Bachelard's use of phenomenology and Sartre's, see François Pire, De l'imagination poétique dans l'œuvre de Gaston Bachelard (Paris: José Corti, Paris, 1967), pp. 151–91.

ness; it allows Bachelard to renew his warnings against the temptation to study images as *things*. Images are "lived," "experienced," "re-imagined" in an act of consciousness that restores at once their timelessness and their newness.

Therefore, a poetic image does not duplicate present reality, and is not the echo of the past; it can be provoked by occasional circumstances, but it has no true causes. The best way to study images is to explore their power of trans-subjectivity. They *reverberate* in the reader's consciousness and lead him to create anew while communicating with the poet. [16]

Despite an apparently clear opposition between Bachelard's *psychoanalytical* and *phenomenological* books, it would be artificial to divide his work into two methodological phases. In fact, his description of reverie is phenomenological throughout his early work (e.g., TV: 114); later, he never repudiates the function of material elements since they possess archetypal energy. Because he restates the requirements of a methodology of imagination, this moment of self-criticism helps the reader to see more clearly what was essential in the preceding books. The fundamental problem remains the same, constituting a "minor cultural crisis" for the rationalist. The understanding of images is paradoxical since we always try to understand by relating the new to the old, the particular to the general. "How can an image, at times very unusual, appear to be a concentration of the entire psyche?" Bachelard asks. "How – with no preparation – can this singular, short-lived event constituted by the appearance of an unusual poetic image, react on other minds and in other hearts, despite all the barriers of common sense, all the disciplined schools of thought, content in their immobility?" (PE: 3). Bachelard expresses here the central difficulty of aesthetics, for any work of art has two poles: the presence of a singular being and the ideality of

16   This is the aspect of Bachelard's thought that Georges Poulet, in his essay, "Bachelard et la conscience de soi," appreciates most. Mikel Dufrenne believes that Bachelard is playing a dangerous game when he infuses the author's images with his own reveries. See his "Critique littéraire et phénoménologie," *Revue internationale de Philosophie* 68–69 (1964): 193.

communicable meanings. Poetry is that zone of language in which originality is impregnated with potential universality.

Language

In agreement with the major trends of modern linguistics, the philosophy of language implicit in Bachelard's poetics postulates that meaning does not precede words. [17] "One would not be able to meditate in a region that preceded language," according to Bachelard (PE: 7). Language is not only a source of meaning, it is also a source of being. The opening to the world by *logos* is at the same time the creation of the world. Whereas Bergson sees in the necessity of words a reduction of spiritual richness to the limitations of space, Bachelard discovers in language a temporal process through which imagination becomes the "humanizing faculty par excellence" (AS: 20). To imagine is therefore to encounter "the speaking being's creativeness" (PE: 8). Literary expression, and particularly poetry, contains for Bachelard the essential characteristics of imagination. Indeed, images are not primarily visual, auditive, or tactile: they are spoken. Better still, they are written in solitude because declamation threatens the inductive power of words; it does not allow the slow and repetitive rhythm that reverie requires. "Truly, words dream" (PR: 16). On the semantic level, Bachelard defines the imaginative power of words as inductive magic. In poetry, words regain their potentialities for dual meanings. They attract one another and create relations that reverse the real and the figurative poles. There is actually no figurative meaning: "All figurative meanings retain a certain sensory density" (ER: 198). In fact, the semantic properties of language cannot be separated from its physical properties. Bachelard describes in many instances the *correspondence* between the materiality of things and the materiality of words.

17   Commenting on the work of Ferdinand de Saussure, Merleau-Ponty writes: "There is thus an opaqueness of language. Nowhere does it stop and leave a place for pure meaning; it is always limited only by more language, and meaning appears within it only set in a context of words." *Signs*, trans. Richard McCleary (Evanston: Northwestern University Press, 1964), p. 42.

In a chapter entitled "La parole de l'eau" he shows that the language that speaks of water absorbs "the lesson of the stream"; water becomes a "most faithful mirror of voices" (ER: 258). It is the great teacher of a fluent language, different from the "highly scanned language of authoritarian prosodies" (PR: 49). In this regard, it would be interesting to recall the entire conclusion of *L'Air et les songes*, as well as the chapter "Rêveries sur la rêverie" (PR: 25ff.). In the latter, Bachelard's reverie on the phonetic qualities of masculine and feminine genders expands into a meditation on the androgyny of imagination.

Linguists tend to dismiss the problem of genders [18] while psychoanalysts often relate this polarity to impulses so remote it is difficult to understand how they could be creative at the level of poetic language. But poets are more subtle. They know how to use properties of language that alternate between the hardness of masculine sounds and the softness of feminine sounds. [19] Poetic reverie truly reconciles the two genders in an androgyny that goes far beyond the human sexual duality studied by psychoanalysts. But reverie, by

18   For linguists, the attribution of genders is purely accidental; in general, they separate semantics from grammatical structures. However, Roman Jakobson indicates a different trend in linguistics when he says: "Grammatical meanings, as many linguists have established, and as poetry demonstrates from the beginning, have great importance for our daily life, our emotional life, our poetic life, even for our scientific creations." Interview given to *La Quinzaine littéraire*, no. 51 (May 15, 1968). See also his *Essais de linguistique générale* (Paris: Éditions de Minuit, 1965), p. 244.

19   In PR: 37 Bachelard cites the manner in which Paul Claudel reproaches Flaubert for his monotonous and dominantly masculine harmony, one which fails to make use of "le ballon des féminines, la grande aile des incidentes." In the same chapter Bachelard indirectly suggests that the difficulty of translating poetry derives from the fact that we truly experience reveries in our mother tongue, in the language of "whispering memory" (PR: 26). Transposition to another language therefore forces us to dream differently. He says that after the first shock of discovering the masculine German word *Brunnen*, he accepted it as an original sound for a pure water, although it seemed harder and more diabolic than his familiar *fontaine*. He notes also that the lack of genders in English may cause a corresponding loss in possible dimensions of reverie (PR: 34). However, for Bachelard the androgyny of reverie is broader than grammatical categories. He would probably have accepted the plea in favor of poetic translation made by Georges Mounin in *Les Belles infidèles* (Paris: Cahiers du Sud, 1955), pp. 73–75 and 109–16. For Mounin, a faithful poetic translation is an exercise of parallel reveries in two languages.

virtue of its orientation toward happiness and repose, is essentially an expansion of the feminine *anima*.

Thus the relationship between the image and the unconscious must be contained within the realm of language. Images are not a translation of complexes; rather, it is the imagination that awakens the complex. Indeed, Bachelard gradually abandons the too causal notion of complex, while according more importance to the autonomy of imagination. In this way the phenomenology of the image can be said to illuminate psychoanalysis. Primordial images such as those of flight, falling, and the labyrinth are spoken before they are thought, felt vicariously before they are experienced in life. They elicit the peculiarly lyrical emotion of possible experience.

A Poetic Materialism

We must bear in mind that Bachelard's research was guided by his enthusiasm and respect for the life of the imagination, for what he calls the *imaginary*. He constantly points to the danger of going beyond the realm of images. Images belong to humanity; they lead to no celestial vision. There is no trace of any Orphic mysticism in his study. He also suggests limits in the exploration of subjective depths expressed by poetry. The critic must not descend into the unconscious to the point of losing the new image within organic or biographical explanations. Bachelard's area of interest is thus a large intermediary zone closed to any transcendence.

Since Bachelard directs his psychoanalysis toward the archetypal aspects of the material universe rather than the subjective pressures of an individual past, his poetics rests on a personal form of materialism. Classical philosophy has accustomed us to an antithesis between matter and form, with only the latter comprehended by spirit. In contrast, for Bachelard, matter becomes the provocation of a basic relationship between subject and object, and the "mother-substance" of all dreams. This conception of matter is equally distant from the rational materialism of science that excludes the joys of participation, and from the utilitarian realism of our daily life. "Sometimes, even when I touch things, I still dream of an element" (PE: 19).

The immediate advantage of the notion of matter is to provide a principle of individualization through its four fundamental divisions. Bachelard readily accepts this list as the basis of a classification for *oneiric temperaments*. This is perhaps the best known and most controversial aspect of his poetics. The orientation of an individual imagination by one of the elements has for him the weight of "law," expressed at times with a certain extremism. "He who listens to the stream cannot be expected to understand the one who hears the singing of the flame" (PF: 178). One of the tasks of literary criticism is thus to trace in each poet the preferred image that gives a profound unity to his work. Bachelard himself has applied this sort of *reagent* to several poets in order to determine their favorite element. His study of Nietzsche is particularly interesting in that the philosopher-poet borrows his multiple images from all four elements. However, in a long section of *L'Air et les songes*, Bachelard demonstrates that the essential scheme of Nietzsche's symbolism is the ascent in icy cold air. The predilection for a dynamic and pure element is the direct, concrete expression of the philosophy of the superman.

But, as Gilbert Durand – following Sartre – points out, Bachelard's poetic instinct is surer than his system. [20] He is the first to break the too perfect symmetries that he advocates in his most rational moments. Therefore, we must not attribute an absolute value to the law of the oneiric temperaments. As a working hypothesis, it can give rise to penetrating studies, provided it is applied with the extreme freedom and sensitivity Bachelard himself has demonstrated.

Perhaps the most significant aspect of Bachelard's poetic materialism is the consequent devaluation of the imagination of forms, and privilege given to depth over surfaces. Material imagination is "this amazing need for *penetration* that, going beyond the attractions of the imagination of forms, thinks matter, dreams in it, lives in it, or, in other words, materializes the imaginary" (AS: 14).

---

20   Gilbert Durand, *Les Structures anthropologiques de l'imaginaire* (Paris: Bordas, 1969), pp. 25–26, and "Psychanalyse de la neige," *Mercure de France* (August 1953). Another sympathetic criticism of this "law" may also be found in François Pire, *De l'imagination poétique*, pp. 58–70.

Indeed, if we reconsider the last part of the definition of material imagination given above, we notice a significant substitution of the adjective by the verb. Materiality, therefore, is not a superfluous property added to images, not a characteristic quickly attributed to objects; it is the imaginary act itself, by means of which images acquire their density, their worldly weight.

The universe of forms – particularly visual forms – bears the negative sign of fixity. Vision seems confined to the passive perception of surfaces, lines, and colors; it is "the less sensuous sensation." However, vision can become an active contemplation when confronted with a natural element. For example, water is a natural mirror; it offers the possibility of poetic transposition of forms, and it also has a depth that immediately leads the poet to a "cosmic narcissism." The idealized image reflects itself in the subject. Moreover, through the reflection given by nature the whole world tends to beauty; water itself dreams. "Such is the endless dialogue between creative imagination and its models" (ER: 37). This dialogue develops even more freely when one work with materials, when a closer contact with a substance stirs our energy. "The hand also has its dream," and each tool has its unconscious. Matter then becomes the "mirror of our energy" (TV: 23). Work is healthy rivalry; it injects our anger, our hostility, into matter. Each of Bachelard's analyses – of the sculptor, the ceramist, or the blacksmith – is a fascinating illustration of double projection: work elicits dreams, dreams stimulate work. But Bachelard does not mean that the craftsman is necessarily a poet, or that poetry is simply a description of work. In fact, the poet knows, even more than the sculptor, the metaphors of hardness. Poetry is a poesis in the sense that it achieves – or makes – the dream of nature. [21]

---

21   Since for Bachelard poetry is a demiurgic activity, it is difficult to say whether he regards it as the work of man or the work of nature. At times he seems very close to Novalis's idea that man is the speaker for the poetry of nature: "The world imagines itself in human reverie" (AS: 22). But in fact, Bachelard leaves the question open: "When a dreamer speaks, who speaks, he or the world?" (PR: 161).

Dynamic Imagination and the Dynamics of Imagination

It would be difficult to clarify the process of the materialization of images without insisting on the use of the phrase "dynamic imagination." Bachelard's terminology is not always clear; he asserts the fundamentally dynamic nature of imagination, but he also indicates the possibility of a more restricted definition: imagination, when occupied with movements and forces rather than with matter, is dynamic by virtue of its content. [22] It is, however, the larger meaning that is dominant throughout Bachelard's work, since no element can be imagined in a state of inertia. That would involve the negation of imagination, the return to a passive perception of given forms. On the contrary, the imagined element tends toward new forms. "A formal, a dynamic, and a material intention are simultaneously necessary to capture the object in its force, in its resistance, and its matter" (ER: 214). Even in contact with an element as strongly material as the earth, imagination asserts its mobility. The dynamic intention is not simply what produces images of forces, it is that which designates the very freedom of imagination in relation to perception.

It is a truism to say that to imagine is not to perceive – at least this has been so since romanticism granted to the visionary poet supremacy over the keen observer of things. [23]

Bachelard nevertheless feels the need to insist on this point, for the origin of images in perception tends to impose itself as obvious. Imagination, however, is essentially a rejection of the tyranny of forms, primarily of forms given by reality but also of forms evoked

22   This is precisely the case with Lautréamont's imagination. In his books on the elements, one of the "two components" – material and dynamic – dominates in each family of images. For example, in aerial images, movement is more important than matter; air is a poor substance. With water, the image of a quiet lake is clearly material, while images of turbulent water are predominantly dynamic.

23   See, for example, Baudelaire's eulogy of imagination, "La reine des facultés," in Charles Baudelaire, Œuvres complètes (Éditions du Seuil, 1968), p. 1036; his appreciation of Balzac as a visionary writer (p. 692); and his numerous reflections on the danger of slavish observation.

by the imagination itself – of all these fixed images that seem to of-fer themselves to perception. [24]

Imagination creates images, but above all it creates a world that opens anew with each image. Bachelard repeatedly denounces the temptation to favor images over imagination. For example, the sym-bol of the wing is too static to communicate the conviction of airy flight; rather, it is flight's logical embellishment. Perceptive habits as well as linguistic habits produce only superficial beauty, and bright words added to an already apparent meaning neither make a good image nor bewitch us. "A stable and completed image *clips the wings of imagination*" (AS: 8). In this respect, the critic has a double obliga-tion: to detect the images that set the world in motion, and to avoid attributing too quickly a point of departure to this movement.

Bachelard carries this theme to its extreme when he affirms not only that imagination is autonomous in relation to perception, but also that it precedes perception. He even says that it is an *a pri-ori* of any psychological function. This helps us to understand the "Copernican revolution" first enunciated in *L'Air et les songes*. When Bachelard says that terror is present before the monster, and nausea before the fall, he does not consider these emotions to be echoes of a personal past but signs of a life ceaselessly renewed within the soul. Imagination is the source of the formal design of images as well as of the emotion. In this sense, poetry illustrates the metaphys-ics of perception tends to impose creative imagination. Bachelard's phrase "function of unreality" contrasts with "function of reality," which for psychologists designates our adaptation to the world around us. Far from placing imagination in the perspective of men-tal pathology, Bachelard clearly sees in it a power of successful ad-justment. "A being deprived of the function of unreality is neurotic as well as a being deprived of the function of the real ... If the func-

---

24 In considering an abundance of descriptive details to be extrinsic to po-etry, Bachelard's opinion coincides, ironically, with that of the seventeenth-century French critic Nicolas Boileau-Despréaux, although their arguments are diametrically opposed. For Boileau, details blur the clear meaning; for Bache-lard, details are too clear. Flowers, clouds, and colors amuse the imagi-nation but fail to commit it to a "voyage."

tion of opening out, which is precisely the function of imagination, does not perform well, perception itself remains obtuse" (AS: 14). Imagination, even conceived as a free movement, does not lead to delirium; it opens the reality of the imaginary, whose true sign is for Bachelard the emergence of the "happy being." Each new poetic world is not a pure invention, it is a possibility of nature.

Images that properly fuse emotion and symbol operate neither at the surface of things nor at the surface of language. "The poet does not describe, he exalts things" (PR: 163). It is not enough to deform and transform reality. Images are the sign of an *élan* – an indication of excess. Imagination always reaches beyond what is given: it magnifies and deepens, it gathers the whole world into a simple image and the whole subject within its reverie. In this way Bachelard expresses, independently, an idea of contemporary moralists: humanity realizes itself only by reaching beyond itself. He also renews and refines the romantic philosophy of imagination that links beauty to excess. It is human imprudence that is beautiful.

The Poetic Sphere

Bachelard's poetics may be summarized by grouping its themes around two axes: a positive and a negative one, which are in fact inseparable. Any reduction of images to another reality, physical or psychological, betrays their nature. Therefore, he condemns realistic or intellectualistic explanations. As for the positive aspects of imagination – its dynamism, its precedence over perception, its rejuvenation of old language – such aspects can never be encompassed by a psychology; they require an ontology, a *fantastique transcendantale*, as Novalis indicated. [25]

Although Bachelard asserts that he wants to limit his ambitions to a "metapsychology" of the imagination, it is obvious that he grants

25 TV: 5. In the vocabulary inherited from Kant, *transcendental* is opposed to *transcendent*; the former designates *a priori* conditions of experience. Bachelard places imagination on this transcendental level. For example, the chapter on the "Reveries of Childhood" (PR: 84–123) is not a psychology of memory but rather a "metaphysics of the unforgettable" (PR: 19).

metaphysical qualities to the poetic dimension of human existence. "I would like so much to show that poetry is a synthesizing force for human existence!" (PR: 107). More accurately, his work illustrates a dialectical awareness of determinism and freedom.

We discover in studying the material elements that "imagination is more determined than we think it is" (TV: 211). There is a way to dream well, to dream in agreement with the becoming of an element. Each properly dreamed element is a lesson of maturation: "One does not treat granite with childish anger" (TV: 21). In the same book, Bachelard challenges Sartre's choice of softness, viscosity, and shapelessness as direct symbols of the apprehension of the concrete world by human consciousness. [26] For Bachelard, these are pejorative qualities, images fixed in the moment of their material becoming. Robert Champigny expresses the same opinion when he describes Sartre's images – in Being and Nothingness – as a past frozen on a material tropism. [27] Commenting on the images in La Nausée, Bachelard writes that "Roquentin's sickness is in the very world of his material images" (TV: 113).

The Sartrean subject, then, does not complete the dynamic movement of the image. For the worker who knows how to impose, through kneading and baking, an ultimate state of hardness on the soft dough, viscosity is only "a temporary insult." Healthy and happy reverie prolongs the struggles between water and earth and between water and fire. The baker who seeks the proper proportions of water and flour, the exact coloring of the crust, is an analogue of the poet working on imaginary mixtures and directing them toward the beauty of forms.

---

26   In Being and Nothingness Sartre reproaches Bachelard for the uncertainty of his principles and the excessive use of the notion of projection, but he appreciates the notion of "material imagination" as a great discovery. In TV: 115 Bachelard in turn praises Sartre for having recognized the importance of direct symbolization for a concrete philosophy – for having insisted that the description of nausea in his work is not a metaphor. They both agree that matter reveals the human being to himself; both refuse to explain symbols by sexual reference. Nevertheless, the difference between them is profound. The Sartrean subject is threatened by a viscosity that simultaneously fascinates and entraps him. Bachelard replies, in essence, "the world is my provocation."

27   Robert Champigny, "L'expression élémentaire dans L'Être et le Neant," Publications of the Modern Language Association of America 68 (1953), p. 64.

It is obvious, however, that material elements are not objective determinants of images; they are never separated from human gestures and dreams, without which reality could not be constituted. They allow the expression of human destiny in the variations of its tensions. Bachelard's study of imagination points to an axiology. The vastness of Bachelard's complex thought is contained in a very simple botanical metaphor: "Imagination is a tree" (TR: 300). It is capable of integrating earth and sky, reality and ideal.

It is more difficult to clarify the role attributed by Bachelard to actual experiences in the formation of new archetypes or in the reactivation of the old ones. We have several times alluded to his insistent refusal to consider images as echoes of experience. Nevertheless, many of his incidental remarks indicate that there is a relationship between archetypes and actual life. Some oneiric motifs – such as that of leaven – may lose their strength because they correspond to outmoded practices; furthermore, we are constantly exposed to new images. How can we interpret the wish to penetrate into the "poetico-sphere" of our time? The clearest indication is found in a passage about water: "A parachuted humanity will soon have a new experience of 'the leap into the unknown'" (ER: 223). Here, the word humanity should be stressed. The events of our individual existence may at the most awaken a latent emotion when they are related to a natural element. At the same time, the common technological artifacts of modern life foment a kind of resistance to reverie. "Who can say now: my electric bulb, the way one used to say: my lamp?" (FC: 90). The dream of a small light requires a flame; the flame and the lamp are still vivid images in modern poetry. In particular, they animate floral images in a way that reminds one of Proclus's "praying heliotrope" (FC: 85).

It seems that experience can only bring variations to the primal archetypes provided it does not contradict their fundamental direction, and provided these variations find poetic expression. Language plays an essential role in the delineation of the poetic sphere.

Archetypal orientations grant a stability to the imagination, which gives them infinite variations in return. If the domain of imagination is closed to transcendence, this is only a fixed or "coarse" transcendence. But in reverie, the world opens and rises in the movement of images. In rejecting the causality of prosaic life, in limiting himself to a cultural unconscious, Bachelard finds in depth the aspiration to height. [28] Imagination has a *vertical axis* – the axis of sublimation. The psychoanalyst describes a process of sublimation doomed to failure; for him it can only hide a sensual lust in the guise of spiritual language. He does not see that there is a normal, joyous repression in culture. "Purification alone can allow us to examine dialectically the fidelity of a profound love without destroying it. Although it abandons a heavy mass of substance and fire, purification contains more possibilities, not less, than natural impulses" (PF: 198). For Bachelard, poetry realizes a successful sublimation; it is a source of new life.

Poetry as Surrealism

Bachelard describes with admirable effect the reciprocity of humanity and the world. He shows how specific qualities attached to an element or to any particular archetypal situation are related to the ambivalences and even to the violent contradictions found in poetry.

The rational and social language of our daily life attributes definite qualities to certain objects and opposes, without hope for conciliation, black and white, light and heavy, fire and water. What is, then, the poetic truth of "humid fire," of "black milk"? In reverie, which abolishes distances, imagination immediately appropriates a substance before playing with its sensory qualities. "Night is no longer a draped goddess ... ; the Night is made of night, night is substance, night is a nocturnal matter" (ER: 137). Through this somewhat redundant insistence Bachelard wants to show that the language of reverie proceeds from substantives to adjectives; conversely, we must detect the noun hidden within each adjective. [29]

---

28 See Maurice-Jean Lefèbvre, "De la science des profondeurs à la poésie des cimes," *Critique* (January 1964). This aspect of Bachelard's dialectic has also been a major influence on the work of Jean-Pierre Richard. The main theme of his *Poésie et profondeur* is the interplay of depth and freedom in modern poetry.
29 For Bachelard each element possesses specific qualities that require par-

What, for example, is milky water in the moonlight? If the image were frozen in its picturesque characterization, one could easily interpret it as a simple reminder of the color of milk. However, images proliferate in transition from depth to surface. If this whiteness evokes warmth and peace, if it excludes the violence and the coldness of a torrent, it is because water is perceived as a peaceful and enveloping element. It gains the affective qualities of milk, it becomes a white nocturnal matter. Therefore, it is at the level of substances, through their affective values, that relations are possible, that a *soul state* produces a landscape. "Matter is the unconscious of form" (ER: 70).

Somewhat paradoxically, the choice of a particular aspect of matter is analogous to the expansion of subjectivity. Here psychoanalysis is helpful in that it provides an inventory of the primordial images shared by many souls. For instance, water is unmistakably a feminine element. But Bachelard does not operate with such generalizations, for the unconscious does not recognize itself in a global and massive element; contradictions within matter are the true principles of individualization. Such a conception helps us to understand in what way one "poet of water" is to be distinguished from another "poet of water." Indeed, Bachelard divides and subdivides each element: the heavy and dormant water of Poe's poetry is opposed to the violent and energizing sea that inspires Swinburne's lines. Bachelard even felt compelled to write two separate books about aspects of the earth capable of stimulating either extroverted dreams of work or introverted dreams of repose. Through an imagined element, dynamic imagination imposes an individual orientation on matter. Each poet "follows the destiny" of a fundamental reverie; material images become the very language of his desires, his fears, his memories.

We must go further if we wish to agree with Bachelard's notion that contradictions are the principle of aesthetic life. Literary criti-

---

ticular approaches. A glance at his chapter headings is revealing in this respect. Water remains more or less similar to itself, and its diversity is expressed by adjectives: calm, clear, heavy, violent. The earth, in contrast, is viewed as different substances: rock, sand, crystal, mud.

cism has gained nothing by tracing the sinister water of Poe's imaginary landscape to the actual lake of Auber, which is linked to the death of his mother. It is within the imaginary element that the dynamics of values must be studied. A value is not something already achieved, it is a becoming, an aspiration. In Poe's poetry, water aspires to death by absorbing darkness, immobility, silence; it becomes "the matter of despair." Moreover, every value evokes its opposite and is in constant struggle with it. Bachelard finds in poetry an application of the philosophy of values that insists on their precariousness. "Better than anyone else, a farmer knows the value of pure water because he knows that its purity is in danger" (ER: 188). Poetic language expresses the continuous tension within a substance. It is by virtue of the dialectic of opposite qualities that poetic matter fascinates us. It is not absurd to speak of the blackness of milk, if one feels that white becomes white by repulsing darkness. Modern poetry, from which Bachelard draws a great number of his examples, succeeds especially well in suggesting tenderness through non-sense. Such quality exists in a kind of vibrating duration. Imagination not only sees a substantive within an adjective, it also finds a verb concealed under each word. [30]

In addition, poetic contradictions become alive when they require the participation of the entire subject. Bachelard favors images that engage all our senses. Contradictions are more than mere tolerance of judgment for unusual associations: they express the need to displace facts by values. "In darkness the attentive ear tries to see" (TR: 87). Bachelard expands the well-known theory of *correspondances*, which he thinks more faithful to the dynamism of imagination than Rimbaud's alchemy. "A doctrine of imagined qualities must not only achieve the Baudelairean synthesis by adding to it the deepest organic aspects of consciousness, it must also emphasize a daring, proliferating sensuousness, intoxicated with inexactitude" (TR: 81).

---

30   Whenever possible, Bachelard uses an active word (verbal adjective or present participle) instead of a noun. For example, he speaks of a "rêverie pétrifi-ante" instead of the expected "rêverie de la pierre" in his discussion of Huysmans's work in TV: 205.

This is a sufficient reason to devaluate those metaphors that simply replace one object with another, a thought with an image.

Although Bachelard does not state it expressly, the necessity of dialectic contradictions takes on a greater importance in his work than the "law of the four elements." If he allows his classifications to overlap, or superimposes one dialectic on another, he thereby illustrates his unwillingness to establish a definitive system. He is less interested in the structure of dreams than in the constant discovery of surprising poetic relationships that enrich the world. "Images are incapable of repose" (PS: 36). They must be studied simultaneously as isomorphic and unique. Images of the nest, the house, and the grotto communicate through a profound dream of security and protection, a dream that evidently evokes the return to a maternal element. But the psychoanalyst who reduces them to unity projects his clear consciousness upon the unconscious, thereby destroying the originality of the variations. "It would be too simple if the greatest of all archetypes, that of the mother, obliterated the life of all the others" (TR: 122). [31] The cellar and the attic do not offer the same shelter. The critic must be cautious when relating the multiplicity of images to a single theme. One of Bachelard's most repeated admonitions is to multiply the occasions of minute differentiations. Like a star, reverie radiates from a center.

Therefore the objects that offer the best pretexts for poetry are those that encourage a dialectic of opposites: a bud, a gem, a drawer. They contain in their smallness the potentialities of immense expansion. The house from cellar to attic is a complete and full cosmos. Bachelard devotes his last book of solitary meditation to the single example of a modest candle, which concentrates past and present, as well as the whole world, in its flame. We might find a possibility of reconciliation between the assertion "To perceive and

31   On this subject Bachelard has been misinterpreted by René Etiemble, who asks, in his Le Mythe de Rimbaud (Paris: N.R.F., 1952), p. 385, "Will we believe ... that 'le pavillon en viande saignante' ... means for Gaston Bachelard the womb of Madame Rimbaud, in which Arthur wants to find refuge?" In fact, Bachelard simply suggests that such an image corresponds to "the oneirism of the house-body" (TR: 127).

to imagine are as antithetic as presence and absence" (AS: 10) and the personal confession that follows it, "O my things, how we have talked!" Memory is the continuation of this dialogue. Through these dreamed objects, the reverie of childhood restores not the objective past but permanent childhood. On several occasions Bachelard says that true images are "engravings," remembrances engraved by the imagination on memory. "Space contains compressed time" (PS: 8).

Bachelard's poetics opens into an ethic of joy, one to which I have already alluded several times. In particular, *La Poétique de l'espace* celebrates the joys of the round cosmos in which we live happily. But Bachelard's fundamental optimism leads him to favor the vertical axis of reverie: imagination is ascension, tree, flame. "Anguish is artificial: we were meant to breathe freely" (PR: 22).

A Summary of Bachelard's Poetic Art

Bachelard's work does not allow a systematization of his poetic art. However, the texts that follow this introduction contain some significant guidelines for the criticism of poetry:

– Poetry is not a translation of life. To speak of descriptive or narrative poetry would be a contradiction in terms. The essence of poetry is the creation of new images.

– It is futile to look for the antecedents of an image. Any type of explanation, whether its tone is rationalistic, realistic or ironic, can kill the image. However, poetry expresses not the haphazard wanderings of the solipsistic psyche but the constant recreation of nature and experience through human speech.

– Poetic sensitivity can nevertheless be educated. The teachings of modern psychology may help the critic to vary his perspectives and his hypotheses, but the best training is achieved through reverie, which puts us in sympathy with words and with substances. The distinction between good and bad taste is of no value. "Good taste is only an acquired censorship" (TV: 338). Bachelard disregards the knowledge of historical sources and influences.

– Images stir and expand the reader's reverie. They *reverberate* in him. Poetic joy is narcissistic. It can be prolonged by a delicate commentary that does not seek to destroy the suggestive magic of images. One of the critic's first tasks is to detect authentic and sincere images. Their criteria, which we may list as ranging from superficial to profound, are: recurrence, inversion of logical categories, proliferation of ambivalences, irradiation with a resulting annexation of other images, and above all the power to offer richer suggestions at each reading.

Bachelard's Place in Contemporary Criticism

By virtue of the heavy emphasis Bachelard places on reverie, his work continues to occupy a prominent place in the dream tradition extending from German romanticism to modern surrealism. Its true originality lies in the recognition of literary imagination as the most complete expression of human imagination.

Although he advocates participation in the creative act, Bachelard does not seek to embrace creation at the level of a complete poetic work. He acknowledges on several occasions his increasing partiality for isolated images. Even his longest monographs (on Lautréamont, Nietzsche, Shelley, Huysmans) display a total indifference to a work's overall structure. In *La Poétique de l'espace* he justifies this somewhat impressionistic method by saying that the genesis and organization of the complete poem are beyond the reach of his modest phenomenological approach: one cannot be in sympathy with the poetic project born in a complex cultural situation. This superb disregard for composition may limit the understanding of creation.

In this respect, Bachelard's place in modern criticism is curiously ambiguous. His conception of a vibrating unity between the elements of imagery is echoed by the modern notion of structures. For Bachelard, however, the teleological orientation of this unity is not the convergence of open meanings within a complete poem but the solitary dialogue between humanity and the world.

Bachelard's sensitive commentaries have nonetheless inspired many French New Critics who do not necessarily share all his predilections. He has broadened considerably the range of critical categories that apply within the realm of images. In particular, he has opened the way to modern studies of poetic time and space: images reveal different ways to live human time and to interiorize objects and distances. [32]

If one had to select a single thought that best expresses Bachelard's poetic outlook on poetry (for he may indeed be said to write poetry on poetry), one that fully suggests its fluid and irreducible nature, it might be this:

> What is the source of our first suffering? It lies in the fact that we hesitated to speak ... It was born in the moments when we accumulated silent things within us. The brook will nonetheless teach you to speak, in spite of sorrows and memories, it will teach you euphoria through euphuism, energy through the poem. It will repeat incessantly some beautiful, round word that rolls over rocks (ER: 262).

Colette Gaudin

Hanover, N.H.

June 1970

32   Michel Mansuy gives a well-documented account of Bachelard's influence in *Gaston Bachelard et les éléments* (Paris: José Corti, 1967), pp. 374–80. Among prominent critics, this influence may best be seen in the work of J.-P. Richard (see note no. 28). Georges Poulet in *Studies in Human Time* (New York: Harper and Brothers, 1956) develops a criticism in agreement with Bachelard's idea of a discontinuous duration. This influence has spread mostly in France, since a very limited part of Bachelard's work is available in translation. Insofar as American criticism is dominated by the influence of New Criticism, it might resist Bachelard's metaphorical approach and accuse it of falling into the *affective fallacy*. As Neal Oxenhandler remarks in "Ontological Criticism in America and France," a rapprochement between French phenomenological critics and the New Critics in America seems impossible. Although there is little direct influence, Bachelard's thought is in harmony with certain important themes of American criticism. For instance, René Wellek and Austin Warren, in their *Theory of Literature* (New York: Harcourt, Brace & World, 1962) draw attention to the central function of images in literature, and Northrop Frye bases the theory of his *Anatomy of Criticism* (Princeton, N.J.: Princeton University Press, 1957) upon the concept of the archetype.

NOTE ON THE TEXTS

The source of each of the following selections from Bachelard's works is identified by the page reference immediately following the selection heading; the abbreviations used are explained in the bibliography. All headings, subheadings, and headnotes are my own. Line breaks within a particular section indicate either that it has been taken from two sources or that a page or more of the original passage has been omitted. Shorter omissions are marked by ellipses.

Bachelard's annotation has been retained, amplified within brackets when necessary, and renumbered in sequence with my own notes, which are entirely within brackets. In general I have attempted to provide a dual system of references. I have cited English translations – when available – of the works in French to which Bachelard refers. When he quotes from English or American literature, I have reproduced the originals in the selections that follow. When he includes quotations from the literatures of other languages, I have endeavored to cite either good English translations or the original sources. In the case of the latter, and also in those instances in which no secondary references are provided, the translations into English are my own.

I wish to express my gratitude to the colleagues who encouraged and helped me as I prepared this edition. I am particularly indebted to John A. Rassias and David Sices for the time and enlightened interest they devoted to this project at crucial stages of its development.

C.G.

I

TWO ASPECTS OF A CAREER: SCIENCE AND POETRY

The Permanence of Reverie

PF: 9–15

We have only to speak of an object to consider ourselves objective. But, by our first act of choice, the object designates us more than we designate it, and what we consider our fundamental thoughts about the world are often an avowal of our immaturity of mind. At times we marvel at a chosen object; we amass hypotheses and reveries; we thus form convictions that have the appearance of knowledge. But their initial source is impure: the primary evidence is not a fundamental truth. Indeed, scientific objectivity is possible only after one breaks with the immediate object, rejecting the temptation of the initial choice, checking and contradicting the thoughts aroused by the first observation. Any objective method, duly verified, belies the initial contact with the object. It must first scrutinize everything: sensation, common sense, even the most constant experience, etymology itself, for the word, which is meant to sing and to charm, seldom coincides with thought. Objective thought does not gaze in wonderment: it must be ironic. Without this critical vigilance, we will never take a truly objective attitude. In the examination of men, equals, or brothers, sympathy is the basis of the method. But confronted with this inert world that is not imbued with our life, that suffers none of our sorrows, and that is exalted by none of our joys, we must halt all effusion, we must restrain ourselves unmercifully. The axes of poetry and science are opposed from the start. All that philosophy can hope is to make poetry and science complementary, to unite them as two well-chosen contraries. We must thus oppose to the poetic mind's effusiveness the taciturnity of the scientific mind, for which preliminary antipathy is a healthy precaution.

I shall study a problem in the context of which the objective approach has never achieved fulfillment, and the initial fascination is so permanent that it can still warp the most upright minds and keep leading them back into the poetic fold where reveries replace thoughts and poems hide theorems. It is the psychological problem posed by our convictions about fire. This problem seems to me so directly psychological that I do not hesitate to speak of a psychoanalysis of fire.

In a book that appeared some time ago, [1] I tried to describe, in connection with calorific phenomena, a well-defined axis of scientific objectivation. I showed how geometry and algebra gradually contributed their abstract forms and principles to directing experimentation onto a scientific path. Now it is the opposite axis – no longer the axis of objectivation but of subjectivity – that I would like to explore in order to give an example of the dual perspectives that could be applied to all the problems posed by the study of any particular reality, however well defined. If I was right concerning the real implication of subject and object, a clearer distinction should be made between the pensive man and the thinker, although without any hope of ever completing this distinction. In any case, it is the pensive man whom I wish to study here, the pensive man sitting by his hearth, in solitude, when the fire is as bright as if it were the consciousness of his solitude.

A task like mine is incompatible with a historical plan. In fact, the long-standing conditions of reverie are not eliminated by contemporary scientific education. The scientist himself, upon leaving his work, goes back to primal valorizations. [2] It would therefore be

1   Gaston Bachelard, Étude sur l'évolution d'un problème de physique: la propagation thermique dans les solides (Paris: Vrin, 1928).

2   [The French word valorisation has recently been borrowed by philosophers from the field of economics. It figures as a neologism among the entries of the Vocabulaire technique et critique de la philosophie, ed. André Lalande (Paris: Presses Universitaires de France, 1950) where it is defined as "the act of acquiring or attributing a value." Valorisation and valoriser are keywords in Bachelard's

useless to describe, along historical lines, a thought process that repeatedly contradicts the teachings of scientific history. On the contrary, I shall devote part of my efforts to showing how reverie constantly goes back to primal themes, operating constantly as a primitive soul in spite of the triumphs of elaborated thought and against the very teachings of scientific experiment.

Furthermore, I shall not settle on a remote period in which it would be only too easy to depict the idolatry of fire. What seems interesting to me is simply to bring out the hidden permanence of this idolatry. Then, the more contemporary the document I use, the more force it will have to demonstrate my thesis. What I am looking for in history is this permanent document, the evidence of a resistance to psychological evolution: the old man within the young child, the young child in the old man, the alchemist behind the engineer.

The Polarity of Imagination and Reason

PR: 45–47

If I had to sum up an irregular and busy career marked by books of different sorts, it would be best to place it under the contradictory masculine and feminine signs of the concept and the image. Between *concept* and *image* there is no possibility of synthesis. Nor indeed of filiation. Especially not that sort of filiation, always spoken of but never experienced, by which psychologists derive the concept from the plurality of images. Anyone who devotes his whole mind to the concept and his whole soul to the image is well aware that concepts and images develop along two divergent lines of spiritual life. It might even be a good idea to stir up competition between conceptual and imaginative activity. In any case, all efforts to make them cooperate are doomed to disappointment. The image cannot give matter to the concept; the concept, by giving stability to the image, would stifle its existence.

---

works. They refer to the spontaneous activity of imagination attributing subjective values to its objects. The frequent use of these terms leads me to retain them in the form of English neologisms: *valorization* and, later, *to valorize*.]

I will not try to weaken the clear polarity of intellect and imagination by resorting to misleading interrelationships. I once felt called upon to write a book in order to exorcise the images that tend to generate and sustain concepts in a scientific education. [3] When the concept assumes its essential activity, when it functions in a field of concepts, the use of images would certainly weaken or even feminize it. Inter-concepts develop within this strong fabric of rational thought – concepts that derive their meaning and their consistency solely from their rational relationships. I have given examples of these inter-concepts in my work, *Le rationalisme appliqué*. In scientific thought, the concept functions better when it is divorced from any trace of imagery. When it is operating fully, the scientific concept is freed from all the slow stages of its genetical evolution; this evolution then becomes a simple matter of psychological study.

The *virility* of knowledge grows with each victory of constructive abstraction, whose action is quite different from that described in books on psychology. The organizational power of abstract thought in mathematics is obvious. As Nietzsche says, "In mathematics ... *absolute knowledge* has its Saturnalia." [4]

The man who devotes himself enthusiastically to rational thought can ignore the smoke and fog by which the irrationalists try to dim the active light of well-organized concepts.

Fog and smoke, the objection of the feminine.

But, on the other hand, I will not speak of my faithful love for images and then study them with the help of a great array of concepts. Intellectual criticism of poetry will never led to the center where poetic images are formed. We must avoid ordering the image as a hypnotist orders his somnambulist subject. [5] To experience the dis-

---

3   Gaston Bachelard, *La Formation de l'esprit scientifique: Contribution à une psychanalyse de la connaissance objective* (Paris: Vrin, 1938).
4   Friedrich Nietzsche, *La Naissance de la philosophie à l'époque de la tragédie grecque*, trans. Genevieve Bianquis [Paris: Gallimard, 1951], p. 205.
5   [Johann Wilhelm] Ritter [(1776–1810), one of the German romantic physicists studied by Albert Béguin], wrote to Franz von Baader [(1765–1941), the most influential of the romantic popular scientists]: "Everyone has within himself his own somnambulist, of whom he is the mesmerist." Quoted by Béguin, *L'âme romantique et le rêve* [Paris: José Corti, 1939], p. 76. When reverie

covery of images, it is better to follow somnambulist reverie, to listen, as Charles Nodier does, to the somniloquy of a dreamer. [6] The
image can only be studied through the image, by dreaming images
as they gather in the state of reverie. It is a contradiction in terms to
try to study the imagination objectively, since one receives the image
only if one admires it. Even the very act of comparing one image with
another risks the loss of contact with their individualities.

Thus images and concepts are formed at opposite poles of mental
activity: imagination and reason. A polarity of exclusion plays between them, in a way utterly unlike that of magnetic poles. In this
case, the opposite poles do not attract but repel. If one loves concepts and images, the masculine and feminine poles of the psyche,
one must love mental powers with two different loves. I understood
this too late. Too late did I come to a clear conscience by working
alternately with images and with concepts: two consciences, one for
daylight, the other accepting the nocturnal side of the soul. To enjoy
my double conscience the clear conscience of my double nature, finally recognized – I would have to be able to write two more books:
one on applied rationalism, and one on active imagination. A good
conscience, no matter how unsatisfactory my works may be, is for
me an *occupied* conscience – never vacant – the conscience of a man
at work till his last breath.

---

is beneficent, when it enjoys favorable continuity, then it is the somnambulist
within us whose orders are imperceptibly carried out by the hypnotist.
6   [Charles Nodier, 1780–1844, French critic and novelist who showed a pronounced predilection for fairy tales and fantastic stories in his critical works.
He was one of the first among the French romanticists to emphasize the mysterious and essential life of the psyche as revealed in nocturnal dreams and in
madness. He is well known for his *Contes fantastiques*, written between 1821 and
1832 (Paris: Carpentier, 1909).]

The Secret of Milk: An Example of Imaginative Synthesis

TR:25–26

...When a poet tells us of the *secret* of milk, he is not lying, not to himself or to others. On the contrary, he is finding an extraordinary totality. As Jean-Paul Sartre says, "we must invent the heart of things if we wish one day to discover it. Audiberti informs us about milk in speaking of its *secret blackness*. But for Jules Renard, milk is hopelessly white, since it is *only what it seems to be*." [7]

Here we can grasp the difference between the dialectics of reason, which juxtaposes contradictions in order to cover the entire range of possibilities, and the dialectics of imagination, which would seize all that is real, and finds more reality in what is hidden than in what is visible. The movement of the dialectics of juxtaposition is opposite to that of the dialectics of superposition. In the former, synthesis serves to reconcile two contrary appearances. Synthesis is a final step, whereas in total imaginative apprehension of form and matter, synthesis comes first: the image that comprehends the entire matter subsequently divides in accordance with the dialectics of depth and appearance. The poet who communicates immediately with the deep material image knows well that an opaque substance is necessary to sustain such delicate whiteness. Brice Parain is right in comparing Audiberti's image with this sentence by Anaxagoras: "Snow composed of water is black, despite our eyes." [8] Indeed, what credit would snow deserve for being white if its matter were not black, if it did not come from the depths of its hidden being to crystallize into its whiteness? The will to be white is not given to a ready-made color, which has only to be kept as it is. Material imagination, which

---

7   Jules Renard, "L'homme ligoté," *Messages II* (1944). [Reprinted in "L'homme ligoté. Notes sur le *Journal de Jules Renard,*" *Situations I* (Paris: Gallimard, 1947), p. 306. Jacques Audiberti (1899–1965) is a modern French poet and playwright and Jules Renard (1864–1910) a French novelist in the realist tradition.]

8   [Anaxagoras, fragment 46A–97 in *Die Fragmente der Vorsokratiker*, ed. Hermann Diels (Berlin, 1912). Quoted by Brice Parain, *Recherches sur la nature et les fonctions du langage* (Paris: Gallimard, 1942), p. 67.]

always has a demiurgic tonality, would create all white matter from dark matter and overcome the entire history of blackness. These expressions may seem gratuitous or false to clear thought. But the reverie of material intimacy does not follow the laws of denotative thought. It seems that we could in some way parallel Parain's very interesting thesis on language by giving to the demonstrating *logos* a certain depth in which myth and image can subsist. Images also *demonstrate*, in their own way. And the best proof that their dialectic is objective is that we have just seen an *unlikely image* impose itself on the conviction of the most diverse writers.

II

CREATIVE IMAGINATION
AND LANGUAGE

The Necessity of Material Causes in Aesthetics

ER: 1–4

Let us help the hydra expel its mist.
– Stéphane Mallarmé, *Divagations*

The image-producing forces of our mind develop along two very different lines.

The first take wing when confronted by the new; they take pleasure in the picturesque, in variety, in the unexpected event. The imagination to which they give life always finds a springtime to describe. In nature, far removed from us, they produce already living flowers.

The other forces that produce images plumb the depths of being; there they seek at once the primitive and eternal. They rise above seasons and history. In nature, within ourselves and without, they produce seeds, seeds in which form is buried in a substance, in which form is *internal*.

To speak immediately in philosophical terms, one might distinguish two imaginations: that which gives life to the formal cause, and that which gives life to the material cause – or, more concisely, *formal imagination* and *material imagination*. These latter concepts, expressed in abridged form, seem indeed indispensable to a complete philosophic study of poetic creation. A sentimental cause, a cause of the heart, must become formal before it can assume verbal variety, before it can become as changeable as light in its many colorations.

But in addition to the images of form so often used by psychologists of the imagination, there are – as I shall show – images of matter, *direct* images of *matter*. Vision names them, but the hand knows them. A dynamic joy touches them, kneads them, makes them lighter. One dreams these images of matter substantially, intimately, rejecting forms – perishable forms – and vain images, and the becoming of surfaces. They have weight, they are a heart.

There are, of course, works in which the two image-producing forces cooperate; indeed, it is impossible to separate them completely. The most mobile, the most changing reverie, the one entirely given over to forms, nonetheless keeps a ballast, a density, a slowness, a germination. On the other hand, any poetic work that descends deeply enough into the germ of being to find the solid constancy and fine monotony of matter, any poetic work that derives its force from the vigilant action of a substantial cause, must still flower, must adorn itself. For the initial seduction of the reader, it must embrace the exuberance of formal beauty.

As a result of this need to seduce, the imagination most often operates where joy goes – or at least where a joy goes! – in the direction of forms and colors, of varieties and metamorphoses, of the probable shapes of future surfaces. It deserts depth, intimacy with the substance, volume.

Nevertheless, I would especially like to focus my attention in this work on the intimate imagination of these vegetative and material forces. Only an iconoclastic philosopher can undertake that heavy task: detaching all the suffixes from beauty, seeking out behind the visible images the hidden one, going to the very root of the image-producing force.

In the heart of matter there grows an obscure vegetation; in the night of matter black flowers blossom. They already have their velvet and the formula of their scent.

When I began my meditation on the concept of the beauty of matter, I was immediately struck by the absence of *material cause* in aesthetic philosophy. It seemed to me, in particular, that the individualizing power of matter was underestimated. Why is the notion of the individual always attached to the notion of form? Is there not an

individuality in depth that makes matter, even in its smallest particles, always a totality? Contemplated in the perspective of its depth,
matter is not merely the lack of a formal activity; it is precisely the
principle that can detach itself from form. It remains itself in spite
of any deformation or fragmentation. Furthermore, matter can be
imbued with values oriented in two directions: in the direction of
depth, and in the direction of height. In the former, it appears as
something unfathomable, as a mystery. In the latter, it appears as an
inexhaustible force, as a miracle. In both cases, meditation on matter develops an *open imagination.*

It is only after studying forms and attributing them to their proper matter that we may envisage a complete doctrine of the human
imagination. We will then be able to understand that an image is
a plant that needs earth and sky, substance and form. The images
invented by men evolve slowly, laboriously, and we understand the
profound observation of Jacques Bousquet: "An image costs as much
labor to humanity as a new characteristic to a plant." [1] Many attempted images cannot live because they are but formal play, because they are not really adapted to the matter they are to adorn.

I believe therefore that a philosophical doctrine of the imagination must first of all study the relations between material causality
and formal causality. This problem confronts the poet as well as the
sculptor. Poetic images, too, have their matter.

Matter is Dreamed and Not Perceived

TV: 3–4

Our long debate concerning the function of the image is stirred up
again when we consider the imagination of *terrestrial* matter. This
time the opposition has innumerable arguments and an apparently
invincible thesis: for the philosophical realist, as well as for the or-

---

1   [Jacques Bousquet is a contemporary French critic who published a well-
documented study on the evolution of images, *Les Thèmes du rêve dans la littera-
ture romantique* (Paris: Didier, 1964). His remark quoted here probably comes
from one of his conversations with Bachelard.]

dinary psychologist, it is the *perception* of images that determines the processes of the imagination. In their opinion, we begin by seeing things, then we imagine them; we combine, through the imagination, fragments of perceived reality, memories of experienced reality, but there is no question of ever reaching the domain of a fundamentally creative imagination. To make fertile combinations, one must have seen a great deal. The advice *to see well*, which is the basis of the realists' education, easily overshadows our paradoxical advice *to dream well*, to dream in harmony with the archetypes rooted in the human unconscious.

Nevertheless, I shall devote the present book to refuting this definite and clear doctrine; I shall also try, in a context that is most unfavorable to me, to establish a thesis that affirms the primal, the psychologically fundamental character of the creative imagination. In other words, the perceived image and the created image are for me two very different psychic manifestations, and it would require a special word to designate the *imagined image*. Everything that is said in psychology manuals about the reproductive imagination must be attributed to perception and memory. Creative imagination has quite different functions from those of reproductive imagination. To the former belongs a *function of unreality* that has as much psychological utility as the *function of reality* so often evoked by psychologists to characterize the adjustment of a mind to a reality marked by the seal of social values. Indeed, this function of unreality will rediscover those values connected with solitude. The ordinary reverie is one of its simplest aspects. But we will encounter many other examples of its activity if we are willing to follow the active imagination in its search for imagined images.

Since reverie is always considered in terms of a relaxed consciousness, one usually ignores dreams of definite action, which I will designate as reveries of will. Furthermore, in the presence of reality, with all its force and its terrestrial matter, it is easy to believe that the *function of reality* rules out the *function of unreality*, and easy to forget the unconscious impulses, the oneiric forces ceaselessly overflowing into conscious life. We will therefore have to pay strict attention if we wish to understand the prospective activity of images, if we want to give the image its place even before perception, as a forerunner of perception.

The Copernican Revolution of the Imagination

AS: 19–20

... It must be admitted that fright does not come from the *object*, from the scenes evoked by the narrator; fright is born and reborn ceaselessly in the *subject*, within the reader's soul. The narrator has not confronted his reader with a frightening situation; rather, he has put him in a *fright situation*. He has stirred the fundamental dynamic imagination. The writer has directly *induced* the nightmare of falling in the reader's soul. He rediscovers a primal sort of nausea that is related to a type of reverie deeply engraved in our inner nature. In many of Edgar Allan Poe's stories, we cannot fail to recognize the primal character of the dream. The dream is not a product of conscious life, it is the fundamental subjective state. In these stories, a metaphysician might see in action a sort of *Copernican revolution of the imagination*. Indeed, images can no longer be explained by their objective TRAITS but by their subjective MEANINGS. This revolution is the equivalent of placing

> dream before reality
> nightmare before tragedy
> fright before the monster
> nausea before the fall;

in short, the imagination is sufficiently vivid in the subject to impose its visions, its terrors, its sorrows. If dream is a reminiscence, it is the reminiscence of a state preceding life, of a state of *dead life*, a kind of mourning before happiness. We might go one step further and put the image not only before thought, before narrative, but also before any emotion. A sort of nobility of spirit is associated with poetic fright; this nobility of the sorrowing spirit reveals a nature so primordial that it forever guarantees first place to the imagination. It is the imagination itself that thinks and that suffers. It is the imagination that acts and that is discharged into the poem. The notion of symbol is too intellectual. The notion of poetic experience is too *experimental*. [2] Random thought and experience are no longer sufficient to penetrate the primal imagination. Hugo von Hofmannsthal writes: "You cannot find intellectual or even emotional terms with which to release the spirit of just such impulses as these; here it is an image that sets it free." [3] The dynamic imagination is a primary reality.

On a theme as slight as falling, Edgar Allan Poe succeeds in providing, by means of a few objective images, enough substance for the fundamental dream to make the fall *last*. [4] To understand Poe's imagination, it is necessary to live this *assimilation* of external images by the movement of *inner falling*, and to remember that this fall is already akin to fainting, akin to death. The reader can then feel such empathy that upon closing the book he still keeps the impression of not having *come back up*.

The Choice of Literary Examples

ER: 23–27

I would like to close my general introduction with a few remarks on the nature of the examples chosen to support my theses. [5]

Most of these examples are taken from poetry. This is because, in my opinion, any psychology of the imagination can be illuminated in its *actuality* only by the poems it inspires. Imagination is not, as its etymology would suggest, the faculty of forming images of reality; it is rather the faculty of forming images that go beyond reality, that *sing* reality. It is a superhuman faculty. A man is a man insofar as he

---

2   [Bachelard is playing on the French word *expérience*, which can mean either *experience* or *experiment*.]

3   Hugo von Hofmannsthal, "Entretiens sur la poésie," *Écrits en prose* [Paris: Schiffrin, 1927], p. 160. ["Das Gespräch über Gedichte," *Gesammelte Werke*, vol. II (Vienna: Fischer Verlag, 1951), p. 102.]

4   [In the preceding pages of AS, Bachelard studies passages from Poe's "The Pit and the Pendulum" and "A Descent into the Maelstrom."]

5   [His theses about the nature of imagination, expressed in the beginning of ER and also in PF and L.]

is a superman. A man must be defined by the tendencies that impel him to go beyond the *human condition*. Any psychology of the mind in action is automatically the psychology of an exceptional mind, one tempted by the exception of a new image grafted upon an old one. The imagination invents more than things and actions, it invents new life, new spirit; it opens eyes to new types of vision. The imagination will see only if it has *visions*. And it will have visions if it is educated through reveries before being educated by experience, if experience follows as confirmation of its reveries. As D'Annunzio says:

> The richest events occur in us long before the soul perceives them. And, when we begin to open our eyes to the visible, we have long since committed ourselves to the invisible. [6]

Here, in this commitment to the invisible, is the original poetry, the poetry that gives us our first taste for our inner destiny. It gives us a feeling of youth or youthfulness by replenishing our faculty of wonderment. True poetry is a function of awakening.

It awakens us, but it must retain the memory of preceding dreams. For this reason I have sometimes tried to delay the moment when poetry crosses the threshold of expression; when I have had clues, I have attempted to retrace the oneiric route leading to the poem. As Charles Nodier says in his "Reveries," "the map of the imaginable world is drawn only in dreams. The tangible universe is an infinitesimal one." [7] For some souls, dreams are the substance of beauty. Adam found Eve after a dream: that is why woman is so beautiful.

Armed with these convictions, I was then able to put aside outworn knowledge, formal and allegorical mythologies that survive in an education devoid of life and force. I was also able to put aside countless insincere poems in which dull rhymers desperately accumulated the most heterogeneous and confused echoes. Whenever I relied on mythological facts, it was because I recognized in

6   [Gabriele] D'Annunzio, *Contemplation de la mort* [trans. André Doderer (Paris: Calmann-Levy, 1928)], p. 19. [*Contemplazione della Morte* (Milan: Fratelli Treves, 1925), p. 17.]

7   [Charles Nodier, *Œuvres complètes*, vol. V (Paris: Renduel, 1835), p. 162.]

them a permanent and unconscious effect on the modern soul. A mythology of the waters, taken as a whole, would be simply a history. My intention was to write a psychology, to link literary images and dreams. Indeed, I have often noticed that the *picturesque* impedes both mythological and poetic forces. The picturesque disperses the force of dreams. To be effective, a phantom should not have bright colors. A phantom lovingly described ceases to act as a phantom. To the different material elements correspond phantoms that keep their strength only so long as they remain faithful to their matter, or, in slightly different terms, so long as they remain faithful to the original dreams.

The choice of literary examples is also due to an ambition that, finally, I admit without regret: should my research attract some attention, it ought to offer some means, some devices for renewing literary criticism. That was my intention when I introduced the notion of *culture complex* into literary psychology. I use that term to designate *unreflective attitudes* that control the very operation of reflective thought. In the realm of imagination, they are, for instance, favorite images that we believe to be drawn from the spectacle of the world, and that are but *projections* of an obscure soul. We cultivate culture complexes in the belief that we arc cultivating ourselves objectively. Thus the realist selects *his* reality from reality. The historian selects *his* history from history. The poet, in arranging *his* impressions, incorporates them into a tradition. In its best form, the culture complex relives and rejuvenates a tradition. In its worst form, it is the academic habit of a writer without imagination.

Of course, culture complexes are grafted upon the deeper complexes that have been brought to light by psychoanalysis. As Charles Baudouin has emphasized, a complex is essentially a psychic transformer. [8] The culture complex continues this transformation: cultural sublimation prolongs natural sublimation. To the cultivated man, a sublimated image never seems beautiful enough; he would

---

8   [Charles Baudouin was a Swiss psychologist who applied psychoanalysis to the study of art and particularly to the study of literature. For his definition of the complex, see "Inconscient, complexes, potentiel," in *Psychanalyse de l'art* (Paris: Alcan, 1929), pp. 1–17.]

like to renew the sublimation. If sublimation were simply a matter of concepts, it would stop as soon as the image is enclosed within conceptual lines. But color overflows, matter multiplies, images develop; dreams keep their impetus despite the poems expressing them. As a result, any literary criticism unwilling to limit itself to the static counting of images must be accompanied by a psychological criticism that re-experiences the dynamic character of imagination, tracing the links between original complexes and culture complexes. There is no other way, in my opinion, to measure the poetic forces at work in literature. Psychological *description* is not enough. It is less a question of describing forms than of weighing matter.

In this book therefore, as in others, at the risk of being imprudent, I have not hesitated to designate new complexes by their cultural signs. These signs are recognized by every man of culture. They remain obscure and evoke no echo in the man who lives far from books. The poorly read man would be amazed were we to speak of the poignant charm of a dead woman's flower-strewn body floating, like Ophelia, upon the current of a river. The development of this particular image has not been examined by literary criticism. It is interesting to show how such images – so unrelated to nature – become rhetorical figures, and how these figures can remain active in a poetic culture.

If my analysis is correct, I believe it should help us to move from the psychology of ordinary reverie to the psychology of literary reverie, that strange reverie that is written and indeed forms itself in the act of writing, that systematically goes beyond its original dream and nonetheless remains true to basic oneiric realities. To attain this constancy of the dream that produces the poem, we must hold before our eyes more than real images. We must trace these images born in us and living in our dreams, these images charged with that rich oneiric matter that provides inexhaustible sustenance for the material imagination.

Invitation to the Voyage

AS: 7–13

... Imagination is always considered to be the faculty of *forming* images. But it is rather the faculty of *deforming* the images offered by perception, of freeing ourselves from the immediate images; it is especially the faculty of *changing* images. If there is not a changing of images, an unexpected union of images, there is *no imagination*, no imaginative action. If a present image does not recall an absent one, if an occasional image does not give rise to a swarm of aberrant images, to an explosion of images, there is no imagination. There is perception or memory of a perception, familiar memory, the habit of colors and forms. The fundamental word corresponding to imagination is not *image* but *imaginary*. The value of an image is measured by the extent of its imaginary radiance. Thanks to the *imaginary*, the imagination is essentially *open, evasive*. In the human psyche, it is the very experience of opening and newness. More than any other power, it determines the human psyche. As Blake proclaims, "The imagination is not a State: it is the Human Existence itself." [9] The truth of this maxim will become more apparent if one studies – as I will do systematically in this book – the literary imagination. This verbal imagination, adhering to language, forms the temporal fabric of spirituality and consequently separates itself from reality.

Conversely, an image that leaves its *imaginary* principle and takes on a definitive form gradually assumes the characteristics

---

9   William Blake, *Seconds livres prophétiques*, trans. [Pierre] Berger [Paris: Rieder, 1930], p. 145. ["Milton, a Poem in 2 Books," in *Complete Writings* (London: Oxford University Press, 1966), p. 522. Blake has a prominent place among Bachelard's favorite poets. See AS: 93–98, on Blake's aerial images, and TV: 181–86, on his terrestrial images. The dialectic of rock and cloud summarizes his dynamic imagination; above all, he is the poet of "absolute imagination" for whom the unreal directs the real.

As in the case of Böhme, whose works are another source of inspiration, Bachelard is primarily interested in Blake's interpretation of the human mind as an *élan* toward the invisible; Bachelard tends to disregard the religious mysticism of these two writers.]

of the present perception. Soon, instead of making us dream and speak, it makes us act. This amounts to saying that a stable and completed image *clips the wings of imagination*. It makes us fall from that dreaming imagination that does not confine itself within any image and that could therefore be called an *imagination without images*, as we acknowledge a *thought without images*. Undoubtedly, the imaginary lays down images during its prodigious life, but it always appears to exist beyond its images, it is always a little more than its images. The poem is essentially an *aspiration to new images*. It corresponds to this essential need for *newness* that characterizes the human psyche.

Therefore, the element ignored by any psychology of imagination that concerns itself solely with the constitution of images is an essential one, evident and known to all: it is the *mobility of images*. There is an opposition – in the domain of imagination as in so many others – between constitution and mobility. And since the description of forms is easier than the description of movements, it is understandable that psychology should concern itself right away with the first of these tasks. And yet it is the second that is more important. For a complete psychology, imagination is, above all, a type of spiritual mobility, the model of the greatest, the liveliest, the most living mobility. We must therefore systematically add to the study of a particular image the study of its mobility, its fertility, its life ...

I shall thus disregard static images, the established images that have become well-defined words. I shall also disregard all clearly traditional images – such as the flower images so abundant in poets' herb gardens. They bring to literary descriptions a conventional touch of color. But they have lost their *imaginary* power. There are other images that are brand new. They possess the life of living language. In their active lyricism, we recognize them by an inner sign: they renew the heart and the soul. These *literary images* add hope to our feelings, a special vigor to our decision to be an individual, a tonus even to our physical life. The book that contains them is suddenly a personal letter for us. They play a role in our life. They vitalize us. Through them, speech, the Word, literature, are raised to the level of creative imagination. By expressing itself in a new image, thought is enriched and enriches the language. Being becomes word. The word appears at the highest psychic point of being. The word reveals itself as the immediate mode of becoming of the human psyche.

How may we find a common measure for this invitation to live and to speak? It can only be done by multiplying experiences of literary figures and of mobile images, by restoring to each thing its own movement, as Nietzsche advises, by classifying and comparing the different movements of images, by figuring all the riches of the tropes generated around a word. About every image that strikes us, we must ask ourselves: what is the verbal force this image releases within us? How do we pull it loose from the too stable bedrock of our familiar memories? To acquire a feeling for the imaginative role of language, we must patiently seek, in every word, the desires for otherness, for double meaning, for metaphor. In a more general way, we must record all the desires to abandon what we see and what we say for what we imagine. We shall then have some chance of restoring to the imagination its role of attraction. Through imagination, we forsake the ordinary course of things. To perceive and to imagine are as antithetic as presence and absence. To imagine is to absent oneself; it is a leap toward a new life.

Often this absence is without law, this impetus does not persist. Reverie merely transports us elsewhere without letting us truly experience all the images to be encountered along the way. The dreamer drifts away.

A true poet is not satisfied with this evasive imagination. He wants imagination to be a *voyage*. Thus each poet owes us his *invitation to the voyage*. With this invitation we register, in our inner being, a gentle impulsion that shakes us, that sets in motion beneficent reverie, truly dynamic reverie. If the initial image is well chosen, it is an impulsion to a well-defined dream, to an imaginary life that will have real laws of successive images, really vital meaning. The sequence of images arranged by the *invitation to the voyage* takes on, through the aptness of its order, a special vivacity that makes it possible to designate, in the cases I shall study at length in this book, a *movement of the imagination*. This movement is not just a metaphor. We shall actually feel it within ourselves, usually as a lightening, an

effortless imagination of connected images, an eagerness to pursue
the enchanting dream. A beautiful poem is opium or alcohol. It is
nutriment for the nerves. It must cause a dynamic induction in us.
I shall try to reveal the multiple implications of Paul Valery's profound remark, "the true poet is the one who inspires." [10] The poet
of fire, of water, or of earth does not transmit the same inspiration
as the poet of air.

That is why the sense of the *imaginary voyage* differs greatly in various poets. Certain poets limit themselves to drawing their readers
into the land of the picturesque. They want to find *elsewhere* what we
see about us every day ...

But authentic mobility, the essence of which is to be found in
imagined mobility, is not properly aroused by the description of reality, not even of reality in the process of becoming. The true voyage of
the imagination is the voyage to the land, to the very domain of the
imaginary. By this, I do not refer to one of those Utopias that creates
all at once a paradise or a hell, an Atlantis or a Thebes. It is the journey that interests us, and instead we are given a description of the
stay. But what I want to examine in this book is actually the immanence of the imaginary in the real, the *continuous* passage from the
real to the imaginary. If we could accumulate experiences of image
transformation, we would understand how profound is Benjamin
Fondane's [11] remark: "At first, the object is not real but a good *conductor* of reality." The poetic object, duly energized by a name rich in
resonances, is a good conductor of the imagining psyche. For such
conduction, we must call the poetic object by its name, its old name,
giving it a just sonority, surrounding it with the resonators it will
bring to life, with the adjectives that will prolong its cadence and
its temporal life. As Rilke says, "in order to write a single verse, one
must see many cities, and men and things; one must get to know

10   [Although I could not find this exact quotation in Valéry's writings, it is
the substance of the following: "The poet is recognized– or at least everyone
recognizes his own poet – by the simple fact that he causes the reader to become 'inspired'" "Poetry and Abstract Thought," *The Art of Poetry*, trans. Denise
Folliot, vol. VII of *The Collected Works of Paul Valéry* (New York: Pantheon Books,
1958), p. 60.]

11   [A French poet and essayist, 1898–1944.]

animals, and the fight of birds, and the gestures that the little flowers make when they open in the morning." [12] Each contemplated object, each evocative name we murmur is the point of departure of a dream and of a line, a creative linguistic movement. How often, beside a well, on the old stone covered with wild sorrel and ferns, have I murmured the name of the distant waters, the name of the buried world. How often has the universe suddenly answered. O my things, how we have talked!

The voyage into distant worlds of the imaginary truly conducts a dynamic psyche only if it takes the shape of a voyage into the land of the infinite. In the realm of imagination, every immanence takes on a transcendence. The very law of poetic expression is to go beyond thought. Undoubtedly, this transcendence often seems coarse, artificial, broken. At other times it works too quickly, it is illusory, ephemeral, dispersive; for the reflective being, it is a mirage. But this mirage is fascinating. It produces a special dynamism that is an undeniable psychological reality. We can then classify poets by asking them to answer the question: "Tell me what your infinite is and I'll know the meaning of your universe: is it the infinite of the sea or the sky, is it the infinite of the earth's depths or of the pyre?" The infinite is the realm in which imagination is affirmed as pure imagination, in which it is free and alone, vanquished and victorious, proud and trembling. There the images take flight and are lost, they rise and crash into their very elevation. There the realism of unreality asserts itself. We understand figures by their transfiguration. The word is a prophecy. The imagination is thus a psychological world beyond. It becomes a psychic forerunner that *projects its being*. In my book L'Eau et les rêves, I have collected many images in which the imagination projects inner impressions onto the external world. In the present book, which examines the aerial psyche, I shall provide examples in which the imagination projects the *entire being*. When one goes so far, so high, one finds oneself in a state of *open imagination*. The imagination in its entirety, hungry for atmospheric realities, adds to

12   Les Cahiers de Malte Laurids Brigge, trans. [Maurice] Betz [Paris: Stock, 1923], p. 39. The Notebook of Malte Laurids Brigge, trans. John Linton (London: The Hogarth Press, 1959), p. 19.]

each impression a new image. As Rilke says, the being feels on the verge of being written: "This time, I shall be written. I am the impression that will transform itself." [13] In this transformation, the imagination sends forth one of those Manichean flowers that blur the colors of good and evil, that transgress the most unvariable laws of human values. One gathers such flowers in the works of Novalis, Shelley, Poe, Baudelaire, Rimbaud, Nietzsche. In cherishing them, one feels that imagination is one of the forms of man's daring. One receives from them an innovative dynamism.

Poetry and the Continuity of Silent Language

AS: 282–85

There are also poets of silence who start by shutting off the clamor of the universe and the roar of its thunder. They hear what they write as they write, in the slow measure of a written language. They do not transcribe their poetry, they write it. Let others *perform* what they have created out of the blank page itself! Let others *recite* into the megaphone of public readings. As for them, they savor the harmony of the written page where thoughts are words, where word equals thought. They know before scanning, before hearing, that the written rhythm is sure, that their pen would stop of its own accord before a hiatus, that it would reject useless alliteration, being no more willing to repeat sounds than thoughts. What a pleasure it is to write this way, stirring all the depths of reflective thought. How freed one feels from time in its awkward, jerky, cluttered manifestations. Through the slow rhythm of written poetry, verbs recover their precise original movements. Each verb is re-endowed, no longer with the time of its utterance but with the true time of its action. Verbs that spin and those that shoot can no longer be confused with each other in their movements. And when an adjective gives flower to its substance, written poetry and literary image let us slowly experience the time of its blossoming. Poetry then is truly the first manifesta-

---

13   *Les Cahiers de Malte Laurids Brigge*, p. 87. [*The Notebook of Malte Laurids Brigge*, p. 50.]

tion of silence. It lets the attentive silence, beneath the images, remain alive. It builds the poem on silent time, a time upon which no rhythmic beat, no hastened tempo, no order is imposed. It builds on a time open to all kinds of spirituality and consonant with our spiritual freedom. What a poor thing is living duration compared with the different kinds of duration created in poems! A poem, then, is a beautiful temporal object that creates its own rhythm. Baudelaire evoked this pluralism of temporal modes: "Who among us has not dreamed, in his ambitious days, of the miracle of a poetic prose, musical, without rhythm or rhyme, supple enough and harsh enough to adjust to the lyric movements of the soul, to the undulations of reverie, to the sudden starts of consciousness?" [14] Must I stress that in five lines Baudelaire has expressed practically all the basic possibilities of tempo in the dynamism of prosody, with its continuity, its undulations, and its sudden accents? But, especially in its polyphony, *written poetry* surpasses all diction. It is in writing, in reflecting, that polyphony is awakened, like the echo of a revealing thought. True poetry always has several registers. Thought flows now above, now below the singing voice. In this polylogism [15] at least three distinguishable levels serve to establish harmony among words, symbols, and thoughts. We cannot *dream* images in depth by listening. I have always thought that the average reader gets a better feeling for poetry by copying it than by reciting it. Pen in hand, one has some chance of offsetting the unjust privilege of sound; one learns to re-experience the greatest of integrations, that of dream and meaning, giving the dream time to find its manifestation or sign and slowly to form its meaning.

Indeed, how can we forget the signifying action of the poetic image? Here the sign is not a reminder, a memory, or an indelible mark of a distant past. To deserve the name *literary image* it must have the merit of originality. A literary image is a meaning in the nascent stage; the word, the same old word, appears and is given a new

---

14 "Preface," *Petits poèmes en prose* [(Paris: Société des Belles Lettres, 1952), p. 4].
15 [Since Bachelard uses "polyphony" twice in the preceding lines, he coins the word *polylogisme* on the same model in order to suggest several levels of thought.]

meaning. But that still is not enough: the literary image must be enriched by new *oneiric life*. To create a different meaning and to evoke a different reverie – that is the double function of the literary image. Poetry does not express what remains foreign to it. Even a sort of purely poetic didacticism that would itself express poetry could not give the true effect of the poem. There is no *poetry* preceding the literary image. The literary image does not clothe a naked image, does not give speech to a mute image. Imagination speaks in us; so do our reveries, our thoughts. All human activity desires to speak. When this speech becomes conscious of itself, then human activity seeks to write, to give order to reverie and thought. The imagination is captivated by the literary image. Literature is thus not a poor substitute for any other activity. It accomplishes a human desire. It represents an emergence of the imagination.

The literary image encourages sonorities, which must be called, in a barely metaphorical way, *written sonorities*. A sort of disembodied ear, able to receive unsounding voices, is awakened in writing; it imposes laws that define the literary genres. The act of writing a language with love produces a sort of projective hearing devoid of passivity. The *natura audiens* prevails over the *natura audita*. The pen sings. If we accept this notion of a *natura audiens*, we shall understand the great value of the reveries of a Jakob Böhme: "Now what does the ear do for you to hear that which sounds and moves? Will you say that it comes from the resonance of the external thing that sounds thus? No, it must also be something that takes in the sound, qualitatively identifies with it, and distinguishes between sounds played or sung." [16] One step further, and the *writing being* hears the written Word, the Word created for man.

For one who knows written reverie, who knows how to live, to live fully, as the pen flows, reality is so far away! What one meant to say is so quickly supplanted by what one finds oneself writing, that we realize written language creates its own universe. A universe of sentences arranges itself on the blank page, in an organization

---

16   Jakob Böhme, *Des trois principes de l'essence divine*, vol. I [Paris: Laran], 1802, p. 322. [*Die drei Principien des göttlichen Wesens*, in *Sämtliche Werke*, vol. III, ed. R.W. Schiebler (Leipzig: Verlag von Johann Ambrosius Barth, 1922) , p. 169.]

of images that often follow different laws, but that always observe the great laws of the imaginary. The revolutions that change written universes give rise to more living, less unnatural ones but never obliterate the functions of the imaginary universe. The most revolutionary manifestos are always new literary constitutions. They make us change universes, but they always shelter us in an imaginary one. Moreover, even in isolated literary images, one feels these cosmic functions of literature in action. A literary image sometimes suffices to transport us from one universe to another. It is here that the literary image appears as the most inventive function of language. Language evolves through its images much more than its semantic effort. In an alchemistic meditation, Böhme hears the "voice of substances" after their explosion has destroyed the "hell of astringency," when it has "crossed the threshold of shadows." [17] In the same way, the literary image is an explosive. It makes the ready-made phrases burst suddenly, it smashes the proverbs that roll from age to age, it makes us hear the substantives after their explosion, when they have left the hell of their source, when they have crossed the threshold of shadows, when they have transmuted their matter. In short, the literary image sets words in motion, it returns them to their function of imagination.

Poetic Images Condense Infinite Meanings in Elliptic Associations

---

AS: 286–88

From the standpoint of its will to shape expression, the literary image is a physical reality that has its own relief. More precisely, it is the psychic relief, the multi-leveled psyche. It furrows or it raises; it finds a depth or suggests an elevation; it rises or falls between haven and earth. It is polyphonic because it is polysemantic. If meanings become too profuse, it can fall into wordplay. If it restricts itself to a single meaning, it can fall into didacticism. The true poet avoids both dangers. He plays and he teaches. In him, the word reflects and

17   [From a passage in the second chapter of Die drei Prinzipien, pp. 13–17, in which Böhme describes the birth of substances.]

reflows; in him time begins to wait. The true poem awakens an unconquerable desire to be reread. We immediately have the impression that the second reading will tell more than the first. And the second reading – contrary to an *intellectual* reading – is slower than the first. It is contemplative. We never finish dreaming the poem, never finish thinking it. And sometimes there comes a great line, one charged with such pain or such thought that the reader – the solitary reader – murmurs: on that day, I shall read no further.

Through the internal working of its poetic values, the literary image shows us that the formation of the doublet is a normal and fruitful linguistic activity. Even when a highly developed language is not available to absorb the new meaning, a linguistic sensitivity makes clear enough the reality of the double meanings. These double meanings, these triple meanings, are exchanged in *correspondences*. Double, triple, and quadruple associations would have a better chance of being created if we could strengthen and prolong our impressions by following the reveries of material imagination based upon two or three or four imaginary elements.

But let us give an example of a literary image in which we can feel the action of a poetic triad. It can be found in a passage of a story by Edgar Allan Poe. For me it is precisely one of those opportunities for pause in reading, and I have never finished pondering over it.

Poe, in the story "The Man of the Crowd," contemplates dreamily, at nightfall, the restless crowd of a great city. As the night grows darker, the crowd becomes more criminal. While decent people return home, the night brings forth "every species of infamy from its den." And little by little the ill of the dying day takes on as it darkens the quality of a moral ill. The gaslight, with its impure artifice, throws "over every thing a fitful and garish lustre." And then, the multiple transpositions of this curious image, to which I draw the reader's attention, take over without further preparation: "All was dark yet splendid – as that ebony to which has been likened the style of Tertullian." [18]

18   Edgar Allan Poe, *Nouvelles histoires extraordinaires*, trans. Charles Baudelaire [Paris: Lévy, 1857], p. 57. ["The Man of the Crowd," in *The Complete Works of Edgar Allan Poe*, vol. IV, ed. James A. Harrison (New York: AMS Press, 1965), p. 139.]

If, having experienced in other poems by Poe the favorite image of ebony, we remember that ebony is for him a melancholy water – heavy and black – we shall feel the effect of a first material transposition when the twilight, still airy a moment before, becomes a nocturnal matter, dense and splendid, stirred under the gaslight by evil flashes. Scarcely have these first reveries been formed than the image opens out: the dreamer remembers, as if it were a somber prophecy, the style of Tertullian. Here then is the triad: night, ebony, a style. And at a greater depth, and in a wider dispersion, darkening air – water – perhaps also a metallic wood, then a written voice, a harsh voice, moving as a mass – accentuated like a dark prophecy – a sense of misfortune, of sin, of remorse. What dreams in two lines! What interchanging of imaginary elements! After slowly dwelling in the world of reveries just opened to him, does not the reader's imagination reveal itself as a pure mobility of images? Drastic ellipses are thenceforth possible. Indeed, one night is as black as an implacable style, another night is black and viscous as a sinister chant. Images have a style. Cosmic images are literary styles. Literature is a valid world. Its images are primary. They are the images of the dream voice, of the dream that lives in the fervor of nocturnal quiescence, between silence and murmur. An imaginary life – the true life – begins around a pure literary image. We must repeat the words of Oscar Milosz for the literary image:

> But those are things
> Whose name is neither sound nor silence. [19]

How unjust is the criticism that sees nothing in language but an ossification of internal experience! Just the contrary: language is always somewhat ahead of our thoughts, somewhat more seething than our love. It is the beautiful function of human rashness, the dynamic boast of the will; it is what exaggerates power. Several times in the text of this essay, I have emphasized the dynamic character of imaginative exaggeration. Without this exaggeration, life cannot develop. In all circumstances, life takes too much in order that thought may have enough.

---

19   O.V. de L. Milosz, "La Confession de Lemuel," [in Œuvres complètes, vol. I, ed. Edmond Jaloux (Fribourg: Egloff, 1944), p. 138].

III

PROBLEMS OF METHOD

Method, method, what do you want of me?
Don't you know that I have eaten
of the fruit of the unconscious?
— Jules Laforgue, *Moralités légendaires*

[Bachelard's selection of these lines as an epigraph for *La poètique de la reverie* may be given a double meaning. He clearly rejects a strict and definitive methodology, but the undertone of the quotation suggests the haunting presence of methodological problems. Through the numerous passages in which he reflects upon his approach, Bachelard evaluates the critical attitude in the light of authentic poetic experience. By excluding reductive approaches from his research he progressively delineates the area of appearance and efficiency of images.

Comparing the first and the last texts in this section, one has the impression that Bachelard is concerned with two different aesthetic problems. On the one hand, images are more related than they seem to be; they possess an organic coherence, and criticism can be the objective study of this coherence. On the other hand, each image is a sudden and surprising event, and Bachelard wants to elucidate the conditions of its *reverberation* in the subjectivity of the reader. In fact, the requirement of objectivity never excludes sympathy; it demands mainly that images be studied in their significant unity and not as decorative fantasies covering a reality different from them. —Ed.]

The Poetics of Metamorphoses

PF: 213–15

If the present work could be taken as the basis for a physics or a chemistry of reverie, as the outline for determining objective conditions of reverie, it should provide the instruments for an objective literary criticism – objective in the most precise sense of the word. It should demonstrate that metaphors are not mere idealizations that go off like rockets, displaying their insignificance by bursting in the sky; but that, on the contrary, metaphors evoke one another and are coordinated more than sensations, so that a poetic mind is purely and simply a syntax of metaphors. Each poet, then, should give rise to a *diagram* indicating the direction and the symmetry of his metaphorical coordinations, exactly as the diagram of a flower defines the direction and the symmetries of its floral development. There is no *real flower* without this geometric conformity. In the same way, there is no poetic flowering without a certain synthesis of poetic images. However, this thesis should not be interpreted as an attempt to limit poetic liberty, to impose a logic or a reality – which is the same thing – upon the poet's creation. It is after the event, objectively, after the blossoming, that we think we discover the realism and internal logic of a poetic work. At times, some really diverse images, which we believe hostile incongruous, disintegrative, become blended into a ravishing image. The strangest mosaics of surrealism suddenly take on continuity of movement. A shimmer reveals a profound light; a glance sparkling with irony suddenly has a flow of tenderness: a teardrop on the fire of a confession. Such is the decisive action of imagination: out of a monster it makes a newborn infant.

But a *poetic diagram* is not simply a drawing. It must find a way to integrate the hesitations and ambiguities that alone can free us from realism, allow us to dream. It is at this point that the task we foresee takes on all its difficulty and all its value. Poetry is not born from within a unity; oneness has no poetic property. If we cannot immediately attain ordered multiplicity, we can make use of dialectic, as a shattering noise that awakens sleeping echoes. As Armand Petit-jean notes, "the restlessness of the dialectic of thought, with images or without, serves more than anything else to determine the imagination." [1] In any case, we must above all arrest the impulses of a reflex expression and psychoanalyze familiar images in order to gain access to metaphors and especially to metaphors of metaphors. Then we will understand how Petitjean could write that the imagination is not subject to the determination of psychology – psychoanalysis included – and that it constitutes an aboriginal and autogenous domain. I subscribe to this view: more than the will, more than the vital impulse, imagination is the very force of psychic production. Psychically, we are created by our reverie, for it is reverie that delineates the furthest confines of our mind.

L: 54–57

It takes real courage to establish, at the basis of metric poetry, a *projective poetry*, as it took a stroke of genius to discover, under metric geometry – belatedly – projective geometry, which is really the essential, original geometry. The parallel is complete. The fundamental question of projective geometry is: What are the elements of a geometric form that can, with impunity, be distorted in a projection while still keeping a geometric coherence? The fundamental question of projective poetry is: *What are the elements of a poetic form that can, with impunity, be distorted by a metaphor while still keeping a poetic coherence?* In other words, *What are the limits of formal causality?*

When we have meditated upon the freedom of metaphors and their limits, we perceive that some poetic images can be *projected* on one another with certainty and exactitude. That is to say, in projective poetry they are really one and the same image. I discovered, for instance, while studying the psychoanalysis of fire, that all the *images* of internal fire, hidden fire, of the fire that smolders under the ashes – in a word, of the unseen fire that consequently requires meta-

---

1   [Armand Petitjean, *Imagination et réalisation* (Paris: Denoël et Steele, 1936), p. 23.]

phors – are *images* of life. The projective link is in this case so primal that we can easily translate images of life into images of fire, and vice versa, with the certitude of being understood by all.

The deformation of images must then be designated, in a strictly mathematical way, the *group* of metaphors. as soon as we might specify the various *groups* of metaphors in a particular poetic work, we would discover that sometimes certain metaphors do not work because they have been incorporated into the group in defiance of its coherence ...

To put it more simply, it is by studying the deformation of images that we shall find the measure of poetic imagination. We shall see that metaphors are naturally linked to metamorphoses and that in the realm of imagination the metamorphosis of a being is already an adjustment to the imagined environment. The importance in poetry of the myth of metamorphoses and of animal fables will seem less surprising.

We can find examples of projective, truly primal poetry on almost every page of Paul Éluard's *Les Animaux et leurs hommes, les hommes et leurs animaux*. The title itself shows quite clearly the double possibility of projection. To cite but a single example, let us look at the poem entitled "Fish":

> Fish, swimmers, boats
>   Transform water.
> Water is soft and moves
> Only for what touches it.
>
> The fish proceeds
> Like a finger into a glove. [2]

In this manner, the environment and the being are coherent: water is transformed, it *gloves* the fish; conversely, the fish stretches, fades away, envelops itself. We have the example of an Éluardian correspondence, clearly formal, which it would be interesting to contrast with Baudelairean correspondences, so strongly material. We would thus find new reasons for classifying poets in two large groups:

2   [In Paul Éluard, *Œuvres complètes*, vol. 1, ed. Marcelle Dumas and Lucien Scheler (Paris· Gallimard Bibliothèque de la Pléiade, 1968), p. 41.]

those who live in a vertical, intimate, internal time like Baudelaire, and those who live in a frankly metamorphosing time, swift as an arrow flying toward the limits of the horizon, as do Lautréamont and Éluard – each type of poet of course translating in his own way the life of metamorphosis. [3] In Éluard's work, the metamorphosis is more fluid; even lions are aerial: "And all the lions that I portray are living, light and immobile." [4]

The Oneiric Source of Aesthetics

ER: 5–7

... In order for a reverie to continue with enough persistence to produce a written work, for it to be more than the simple vacuous pastime of a fleeting moment, it must find its *matter*; a material element must give the reverie its own substance, its own law, its specific poetics. And it was not without cause that primitive philosophies often made a decisive choice in this direction. [5] They associated their formal principles with one of the four fundamental elements, which thus became marks of *philosophical temperaments*. In these philosophical systems, learned thought is linked to a primitive material reverie; calm, durable wisdom is rooted in a substantive permanence. And if these simple, powerful philosophies still remain wellsprings of conviction, it is because in studying them we find quite natural image-producing forces. It is always the same way: in philosophy, one can persuade only by suggesting fundamental reveries, by giving to thought its pathway of dreams.

Even more than clear thought and conscious images, dreams are governed by the four fundamental elements ...

In a general way, I believe that the psychology of aesthetic emotion would profit from studying the kinds of material reveries that

---

3   See "Les superpositions temporelles," in [Gaston Bachelard,] *La Dialectique de la durée* (Paris: Boivin, 1936), [pp. 90–111,] and "Instant poétique et instant métaphysique," *Messages* 1.2 (1939).
4   Paul Éluard, *Donner à voir* [Paris: Gallimard, 1939], p. 20.
5   [Bachelard often refers to pre-Socratic philosophers, e.g., "For Heraclitus, death is water itself." ER:79.]

precede contemplation. We dream before contemplating. Any landscape is an oneiric experience before becoming a conscious spectacle. We look with aesthetic passion only at those landscapes that we have first seen in dreams. Tieck was correct in recognizing in human dreams the preamble of natural beauty. The unity of a landscape appears as the fulfillment of an oft-dreamed dream. [6] But the oneiric landscape is not a frame to be filled with impressions, it is a matter that multiplies.

We may thus understand the possibility of connecting a material element like fire with a type of reverie that governs beliefs, passions, ideals, and the philosophy of an entire life. It is meaningful to speak of an aesthetic of fire, a psychology of fire, and even an ethics of fire. A poetics and a philosophy of fire condense all these lessons. Between them they constitute this prodigious, ambivalent teaching that supports the convictions of the heart with the lessons of reality, and that conversely enables us to understand the life of the universe by the life of our hearts.

All the other elements abound in similar ambivalent certitudes. They suggest secret confessions and display brilliant images. All four of them have their disciples, or more exactly, each of them is already profoundly, materially, a *system of poetic faithfulness*. By singing them, we believe we remain true to a favorite image; in reality, we are faithful to basic human sentiment, to a primal organic reality, to a fundamental oneiric temperament.

The Law of the Four Elements

AS: 14–15

... In this essay, I will study the most escapist *imaginary voyages*, the least settled sojourns, these often inconsistent images; nevertheless, it will bee seen that this flight, this instability, and this inconsistency do not preclude a truly regular imaginative life. All of this disorder even seems at times to offer such a defined movement that it can

---

6   Ludwig Tieck, *Werke*, [vol. V (Leipzig: Deutsches Verlaghaus Bong & Co., 1892), p. 21].

serve as a pattern for a *rule of coherence through mobility*. Indeed, our manner of escaping reality points unmistakably to our inner reality. A man deprived of the *function of unreality* is just as neurotic as the man deprived of the *function of reality*. One can say that a disturbance of the function of unreality has repercussions on the function of reality. If the function of *opening out*, which is precisely the function of imagination, is badly performed, perception itself remains obtuse. We must therefore find a regular connection from the real to the imaginary. In order to experience this regular connection, we have only to classify properly the series of psychological documents.

This regularity comes from our being drawn forth in the exploration of the imaginary by *fundamental matters*, imaginary elements whose idealistic laws are as positive as experimental laws. Let me draw attention here to a few recent books in which I have studied, under the name of *material imagination*, this amazing need for *penetration* that, going beyond the attractions of the imagination of forms, thinks matter, dreams in it, lives in it, or, in other words, materializes the imaginary. [7] I thought it justifiable to speak of a law of the four material imaginations that *necessarily* attributes to a creative imagination one of the four elements: fire, earth, air, or water. Certainly, several elements can combine to form a particular image; there are *composite* images; but images have a life characterized by a purer line of filiation. Whenever images appear in series, they point to a primal matter, a fundamental element. The physiology of imagination, even more than its anatomy, is subject to the law of the four elements.

The Dynamic Imagination of Lautréamont

L: 26–29

Struck by this enormous biological production, this extraordinary confidence in animal movement, I undertook a systematic study of Lautréamont's bestiary. I attempted in particular to single out the most significant animals, the animal functions that Lautréamont most clearly sought. A quick statistical survey of the 185 animals of

7   [In PF and ER.]

Ducasse's [8] bestiary gives prominence to the dog, the horse, the crab, the spider, and the toad. But I soon discovered that a more or less formal statistical study would shed very little light on the Lautréamont problem, and that it might even present it in the wrong terms. Indeed, if we limit ourselves to noting animal forms and keeping an exact account of their appearances, we neglect the essential part of the *Ducasse complex*; we forget the dynamic vitality of this production. In order to be psychologically exact, I felt obliged to reconstitute the dynamic value, the *algebraic weight* that gives the measure of the different animals' vital actions. Reliving *Les Chants de Maldoror* was the only way to go about it. It was not enough to *observe* their life. I therefore strove honestly to experience the intensity of Ducasse's action. And only after adding a dynamic coefficient did I recast my statistics ...

For example, in *Les Chants de Maldoror*, the dog and the horse are not sufficiently dynamic to be kept in the first rank. They are external means. Maldoror spurs on a charger, arouses a dog's anger, but he does not penetrate into the heart of animal movement. Nothing in *Les Chants de Maldoror*, for instance, allows us to relive the profound experience of the centaur, that creature so misunderstood by the mythologists of the past – who always saw syntheses of images where syntheses of acts should be seen. Thus in *Les Chants de Maldoror* the horse does not rear up; he transports. The dog hardly exceeds the function of aggressiveness imposed upon him by his bourgeois owner. This is a sort of delegated aggression. It lacks the straightforwardness characteristic of Ducasse's kind of violence. Another proof that the dog and the horse are but external images, seen images, is that they do not metamorphose; their forms do not swell as do those of so may other creatures of the bestiary; the dog's muzzle does not multiply and activate the triple violence of a Cerberus. Neither horse nor dog bears any mark of the teratological power that characterizes Ducasse's imagination. There is nothing in them that is still constantly growing. They represent no monstrous impulsion. Finally, as one can see, animals such as the dog or the horse, in *Les Chants de*

8   [Isidore Ducasse wrote under the pen name of Comte de Lautréamont.]

Maldoror, do not in any way designate a dynamic complex. They do not belong to the cruel escutcheon of the Comte de Lautréamont.

I tried to determine, in addition, if the well-known statement, "As for me, I use my genius to depict the delights of cruelty," [9] might not provide the dominant key to his works. But one again I had to admit that ordinary cruelty, represented by the tiger and the wolf, was lacking in dynamism. The image of the tiger, with its classic cruelty, would rather block the development of the complex. In any case, it seems to me that it is these blocked image that catch the mind of certain readers. As astute a critic as René Lalou, for example, remains outside of *lautréamontisme.* In his opinion, the beautiful sentence that praises the delights of cruelty is soon "diluted in trite expressions." [10] One will not receive this impression of dilution if, instead of starting with massive and ready-made cruelty, summed up in a traditional animal, [11] one restores to cruelty its multiplicity, and disperses it over all the functions of inventive aggression.

The Crab as a Paradigm

L: 37–41

The animal favored by Lautréamont's dynamic imagination is the crab, in particular the "tourteau." [12] The crab would rather lose its claw than loosen its hold. Its body has less bulk than its pincers. If we were to imitate Lautréamont's teratological exaggeration, we might express the motto of the crab as follows: *one must live to pinch, and not pinch to live.*

Since only biological movement is significant in the type of imagination I am describing, sudden substitutions become possible: the crab is a louse, the louse is a crab. "O venerable louse ... Beacon of

---

9 ["Les Chants de Maldoror," in Lautréamont, *Œuvres complètes* (Paris: José Corti, 1938), p. 44.]

10 René Lalou, *Histoire de la littérature contemporaine,* [vol. I (Paris: Presses Universitaires de France, 1941), p. 121].

11 [See L: 10 for Bachelard's critique of La Fontaine's use of animal symbolism.]

12 [A species of of large edible crab, very common in France.]

Maldoror, where do you guide his steps?" [13] Then, fiery pages follow one after another. In the middle of the second chant, there appear those passages, devoted to the louse, which have been taken as tasteless ventures, created in a frenzy of unwholesome and puerile originality, and which indeed are completely incomprehensible in terms of a theory of static imagination – the imagination of completed forms. But a reader willing to accept *animalizing* phenomenology, will read in a different spirit; he will recognize the action of a special force, the thrust of a characteristic life. Certainly, animality is at its peak in its virulence: it pushes, grows, dominates. The blood-loving louse "would be capable, through an occult power, of becoming as big as an elephant, of crushing men like blades of wheat." Therefore, it must be kept "in high esteem, above all animals of Creation":

> If you find a louse in your path, go your way...

> You can pet an elephant, not a louse.

> O louse, with your wrinkled eyeball, as long as the river shed their sloping waters into the abyss of the sea, ... as long as the mute void has no horizon ... , they reign will be assured over the universe and thy dynasty will stretch links of its chain from century to century. I salute thee, rising sun, celestial liberator, thou, invisible enemy of man ...

These passages have often been cited as if they were a parody written by a schoolboy. This interpretation disregards the breadth of an original language, its dehumanized sonority brought to the level of an outcry. Psychologically, it is a refusal to experience that strange myth of metamorphoses, which remains cold and formal in certain ancient authors like Ovid, and which takes on a sudden new life in more recent authors who return unconsciously to primal impulses.

In spite of the lessons of natural history or the wisdom of common sense, we must associate Ducasse's eagle and vulture with the louse and the crab. The talon and the beak, which are adapted to each other in animal nature by a vital synergy, must take on, in an imagination

---

13 ["Les Chants de Maldoror," p. 74. The successive poetic excerpts in this passage are taken from pp. 47, 105–9, and 156–67 of the same work.]

given over entirely to the dynamics of animal movement an imaginative synergy with the claw. The eagle's beak, in Lautréamont's bestiary, is nothing but a claw: the eagle does not devour, it tears. Maldoror asks himself: "Is it my sick mind's delirium, a secret instinct independent of my reasoning, like that of the eagle tearing up its prey, which forced me to commit this crime?" Cruelty can have all sorts of reasons – except need or hunger.

The eagle, like the louse, like the crab, like all the vigorously imagined animals of the bestiary, can change dimensions. If combat is necessary, "it will click its curved beak for joy," it will be come "enormous." Then, "the eagle is terrible, it makes huge bounds that shake the earth." As we can see, this is still the same squandering of force – but always a specific force – which grows proportionately with the obstacle, which must always overcome resistance and produce victoriously the weapons of its crime, the animal organs of its offense ...

... These phantasms are not whimsical contrivances; they are, originally desires for specific actions. They are produced by a motive imagination of great sureness, of astounding inflexibility.

An Oneiric Temperament: Nietzsche

AS: 146–85

Limiting myself almost exclusively to examination of the Poems and of that equally lyrical work, Thus Spoke Zarathustra, I feel I can prove that the poet in Nietzsche explains in part the thinker, and that Nietzsche is indeed the typical vertical poet, the poet of the summits, the ascensional poet. To be more precise, since genius is a class formed of a single individual, I shall show that Nietzsche is one of the special, one of the clearest types of dynamic imagination ...

I would like first to justify the aerial character that I attribute to Nietzsche's imagination. To this end, before the demonstration of my thesis showing the unusual vitality and force of aerial images in Nietzsche's poetry, I shall indicate the secondary nature of earth, water, and fire images in Nietzsche's poetics.

Nietzsche is not a poet of the *earth*. Humus, clay, open and plowed fields do not supply him with images. Metal, mineral, gems, which the "earth poet" loves for their *internal* richness, give him no *reveries of intimacy*. Stone and rock appear often in his writings, but only as symbols of hardness; they retain nothing of the slow life, the slowest of all lives – unusual in its slowness attributed to them by the reverie of *lapidary poets*. For him, rock is not alive as an awful gum issuing from the bowels of the earth.

Soft earth is for him an object of disgust. How he despises things that are "spongy, cavernous and compressed." [14] In this case, it can be objected that I treat as *things* what, in psychological reality, correspond to *ideas*; it will be taken as a good opportunity to prove right away the senselessness of studying metaphors detached from their intention. And yet, the adjective *spongy* contains an image that reveals the depth of the imagination so well that it is sufficient for the diagnosis of material imaginations. It is an extremely sure touchstone: only a passionate lover of earth, an earth poet with a trace of aquatic imagination, avoids the *automatically pejorative* character of the metaphor of *sponginess*.

Nietzsche is not a poet of *matter*. He is a poet of action, and I intend to consider him as an illustration of dynamic rather than material imagination. The earth, in its mass and its depth, offers him, above all, themes of action. In this way, we can find in Nietzsche's works numerous allusions to a *subterranean life*. But this life is a subterranean *action*. It is not a dreamy exploration, a spellbound voyage, as in Novalis's imagination. [15] It is the purely active life, the life of long courage, of long preparation; it is the symbol of an ag-

14 "Des grands événements," [Friedrich Nietzsche,] *Ainsi parlait Zarathoustra*, trans. Henri Albert [Paris: Mercure de France, 1932], p. 184. ["On Great Events," *Thus Spoke Zarathustra*, in *The Portable Nietzsche*, ed. and trans. Walter Kaufman (New York: The Viking Press, 1954), p. 243.]

15 [In an earlier passage (AS: 128) Bachelard shows that Novalis's aerial images are always linked to a terrestrial matter that prevents the dreamer from losing his contact with the earth. In Novalis's writings the crystal is a privileged object since it contains light and matter, sky and earth. The contemplation of a limpid stone reveals to the dreamer a magnificent subterranean world. See Bachelard's analysis of a passage from *Heinrich von Ofterdingen* in TV: 285.]

gressive, tenacious, and alert patience. Even working underground, Nietzsche knows where he is going. He would never consent to the passivity of an initiation; he is directly active against the earth. In many dreams, the anxious dreamer wanders through labyrinths. In Heinrich Stilling's *Heimlich* we can find innumerable instances of a labyrinthine ordeal that has its place among the *four ordeals of elementary initiation*. It is a good example of a *law of the four initiations* (by fire, water, earth and wind) that I want to add to the different *quadrivalences of the material imagination* already grouped in my previous studies. But for Nietzsche there can be no initiation; he is always, originally, the absolute *initiator* whom no one has initiated. Under the ground his labyrinth is straight, it is a secret force *making its way, its own way*. Nothing tortuous, nothing blind. The mole is an animal doubly scorned by Nietzsche. Even underground, in his subterranean work, Nietzsche already knows "the formula for his happiness: a yes, a no, a straight line, a goal ..." [16]

Nietzsche is not a poet of *water*. Of course he does not lack water images; no poet can do without liquid metaphors. But in Nietzsche these metaphors are transient; they do not determine *material reveries*. Dynamically as well, water is too readily servile: it cannot be a true obstacle, a true adversary for Nietzsche's struggling hero. The Xerxes complex, which cannot leave its mark on a poet as cosmic as Nietzsche, is quickly dominated:

> You womanly, wondrous waves
> Are you enraged against me?
> Do you rise up full of wrath?
> With my oar I beat your madness on the head. [17]

How dry and quiet is this *blow of the oar* against the inferior passions, the disorderly agitations, the empty foam! A simple tap of the master's ruler on teasing or disobedient hands brings the pupil back to

16 [Friedrich Nietzsche,] *Le Crépuscule des idoles*, trans. Henri Albert [Paris: Mercure de France, 1920], p. 115. [*Twilight of the Idols*, in *The Portable Nietzsche*, p. 473.]
17 [Friedrich Nietzsche,] *Poésies, Ecce Homo*, trans. Henri Albert [Paris: Mercure de France, 1909], p. 234. ["Wasserfahrt," *Dichtungen*, in *Gesammelte Werke*, vol. XX (Munich: Musarion Verlag, 1927), p. 236.]

the right path. Similarly, the master of himself and of the world, sure of his destiny, says at once to the taunting and turbulent waves:

You yourselves will transport this bark to immortality, [18]

that is to say, into the sky, but not with the soft inflection of lulled dreamers who imperceptibly pass from the water into the air: here, order and movement *go off* like a shot.

On days of rest – infrequently – there can appear vast images of cosmic maternity. These are the links of the dynamic images we have to define. Then, water is beneficent milk for a momentarily calmed universe. Nietzsche calls upon the cows of the heavens in order to draw their nourishing milk and to reanimate the earth. Thus, in the last poem of the collection, there appears a need for softness, shadow, water:

> Ten years gone by
> Not a drop reached me,
> No moist wind, no dew of love
> – A rainless land ...
>
> I once asked the clouds
> To depart from the mountains, ...
> Today I entice them to come:
> Bring darkness about me with my udders
> – I will milk you,
> You cows of the heights!
> Milk-warm wisdom, sweet dew of love
> I pour you over the land. [19]

This relief, this womanly reward – after ten years of cold and pure solitude – serves as an antithesis to the drama of tension. It is not the original *dynamic reverie*. When we have realized that the Nietzschean cosmos is one of *heights*, we will understand as well that the bed of this pacifying water is the sky. For Nietzsche, as in the original mythology, Poseidon is Uranian. *Springs* are rare in Nietzsche's universe.

18   Ibid.
19   "Parmi les filles du désert," [Nietzsche,] *Poésies, Ecce Homo*, p. 258). ["Von der Armut des Reichsten," *Dichtungen*, p. 215.]

The substance of water never goes beyond this power of release. In particular, it never offers a temptation of death and dissolution. How clearly Nietzsche rejects the *cosmos of melancholy*, the cosmos overcast with clouds and rain! "The evil play of passing clouds, of dark melancholy, of veiled skies, of stolen suns, of howling autumn winds."

Demonstrating that Nietzsche is not a *poet of fire* is a more delicate task. A poet of genius calls upon metaphors of all the elements. Besides, fire metaphors are the natural flowering of language. The words' softness or violence finds the fire to express them. Any passionate eloquence is an enflamed eloquence. A trace of fire is always necessary if the metaphors of the other elements are to be lively and clear. Polychromatic poetry is a flame that obtains its colors from the metals of earth. It would therefore be easy to gather numerous documents about *Nietzschean fire*. But, if we look more closely, it can be seen that this *fire* is not really substantial, it is not the substance that imbues and tones Nietzsche's material imagination.

Indeed, in Nietzsche's images, fire is less a substance than a force. It plays its role in a peculiar *dynamic imagination*, which I will attempt to define.

One of the best proofs of the essentially dynamic character of Nietzsche's fire is its usual *suddenness: it is a stroke of lightning. It is thus a projection of wrath*, of a divine and joyful wrath. Wrath is sheer action! Resentment is a *matter* that accumulates. Wrath is an act that defers its own fulfillment. Resentment is unknown to Nietzschean man. On the contrary, how could an act be decisive without being indecisive, that is to say, inspired by a little anger, the anger of a pointed finger? In cases where energy is confronted by a terrible task, Nietzschean man's wrath is so sudden that he is not menacing. The being from whom lightning will strike out can quietly conceal his thoughts:

> He who one day is to kindle lightning
> Must long remain a cloud. [20]

20 [Nietzsche,] *Poésies, Ecce Homo*, p. 207. ["Wer viel einst zu verkünden hat," *Dichtungen*, p. 131.]

Thunderbolts and light are keen weapons, cutting weapons:

> My wisdom became a lightning-flash;
> It cut through all darkness for me with a diamond sword. [21]

Instead of Shelley's light that suffuses and penetrates a clear soul with its soft substance, Nietzsche's light is an arrow, a sword. It gives a cold wound.

In a similar way, when fire is possessed in simple enjoyment as a matter, it is a poor man's property that the superman disdains. "Go out, will-o-the wisp!" That is what "the great, eternal amazon, never feminine or gentle like the dove," says to a soul softened by an internal warmth.

Even the more or less nutritive intuitions produce, in Nietzsche, *energies* rather than *substances*:

> They are cold, these learned men!
> Would that a lightning bolt might strike their food,
> And their mouths learn to feed on fire! [22]

This alimentary lightning is for Nietzsche a sustenance for the nerves. It does not correspond to a fire nurtured in a slow and contented digestion. In the great duality between imaginary digestion and respiration, we must look toward the poetry of brisk and happy breathing to find Nietzsche's creation of poetic values.

It is Nietzsche himself who points out that he is an *aerial poet*:

> Storm clouds – what do you matter?
> To us, free, aerial, joyous spirits. [23]

Indeed for Nietzsche, air is the very substance of our freedom, the substance of superhuman joy. The air is a sort of surmounted matter, just as Nietzschean joy is surmounted joy. *Terrestrial joy* is richness and density – *aquatic* joy is softness and rest – igneous joy is love and desire – aerial joy is freedom.

---

21 [Nietzsche,] *Poésies, Ecce Homo,* p. 222. ["Bruchstücke zu den Dionysos-Dithyramben," *Dichtungen,* p. 224.]
22 [Nietzsche,] *Poésies, Ecce Homo,* p. 240. ["Bruchstücke zu den Dionysos-Dithyramben," *Dichtungen,* p. 242.]
23 [Nietzsche,] *Poésies, Ecce Homo,* p. 232. ["Bruchstücke zu den Dionysos-Dithyramben," *Dichtungen,* p. 235.]

Nietzsche's air is therefore a strange substance: it is substance devoid of substantial qualities. It can thus characterize being as suitable to a philosophy of absolute becoming. In the realm of imagination, the air frees us from substantial, internal, digestive reveries. It frees us from our attachment to matter: It is therefore the matter of our freedom. To Nietzsche, air provides *nothing*. It gives *nothing*. It is the vast glory of nothingness. But is not to *give nothing* the greatest of gifts? The great empty-handed donor frees us from the outstretched hand of desire. It accustoms us to receiving nothing, and thus to take everything. "Is it not for the donor to thank the one who is willing to take?" asks Nietzsche. Later we shall see in more detail how in Nietzsche's works a material imagination of air gives way to a dynamic imagination of air. But we can already understand that air is the true home of the predator. There is that infinite substance that we – through an aggressive and triumphant freedom, like lightning, like an eagle or an arrow, like a majestic and new periods glance. In the air one carries off ones pray openly. One does not hide.

But before developing any such dynamic aspects, I want to show the particular material character of *Nietzsche's air*. For a material imagination, what are often the most hopefully *substantial* qualities of air? *Odors*. For some material imaginations, there is about all the *vehicle* of odors. In the air, an odor has infinity. For Shelley, there is an immense flower, the floral essence of the entire earth. Very often we dream of the purity of air as a fragrance at once balmy and empyreumatic; we dreamed of its warmth as of a resinous pollen, a warm and sweet honey. Nature only dreams of the tonic quality in air: it's closeness and emptiness.

For a true Nietzschean, the sense of smell must give the happy certainty of an odorless air, the confirmation of the immense happiness, the blessed consciousness of feeling nothing. It guarantees the total absence of odors. Nietzsche's scent instinct, of which he so often boasted, it's not an attractive power. It is given to the superman in order that he may flee at the slightest sign of impurity. Nietzschean cannot indulge an odor. Baudelaire, the Countess of Noailles – both of them terrestrial, and this is of course the sign of a different power – dream and meditate upon odors. In their case, fragrances have infinite echoes. They link memories to desires, and the enormous past to an immense, unformulated future. On the contrary, Nietzsche says:

> Breathing the purest air
> My nostrils dilated like wine glasses,
> without future, without memories ... [24]

Pure air is a consciousness of the free moment, of a moment that opens a future. Nothing more ... Nietzschean imagination forsakes odors for the very reason that it separates itself from the past ...

... Basically, for Nietzsche, *coolness* is the truly tonic quality in air, the quality that gifts the joy of breathing, that *endows immobile air with dynamism* – a transformation in depth that is the very life of dynamic imagination. Coolness must not be taken as a mediocre or average quality. It corresponds to one of the most important principles of Nietzsche's cosmology: *cold*, the cold of heights, glaciers, of absolute winds ...

Thanks to cold, the air acquires *aggressive virtues*, it takes on that joyous spitefulness that awakens the will to power. It will to react coldly, in the supreme freedom of coldness, with a cold will ...

In this cold air of the heights, we may find another Nietzschean value: silence. It is not the winter sky with its quietude – a sky "that sometimes leaves even the sun in silence" – opposed to Shelley's sky, so musical that we can say it is music transformed into substance? In *Zarathustra*, "On the Mount of Olives," Nietzsche wonders: is it from that winter sky that I have learned the "long blooming silences"? And when we read in the "Return" "O, how this silence draws deep breaths of clean air," [25] how can we reject the synthesis of substances: air, cold, and silence? Through air and cold, it is silence that is inhaled, that is *integrated* into our very being. This integration of silence is very different from the kind we encounter in Rilke's ever sorrowful poetry. In Nietzsche's works, it has an abruptness that

---

24 [Nietzsche,] *Poésies, Ecce Homo*, p. 263. ["Unter Töchtern der Wüste," *Dichtungen*, p. 195.]
25 [Nietzsche,] *Ainsi parlait Zarathoustra*, p. 260. [Thus Spoke Zarathustra, in The Portable Nietzsche, p. 296.]

destroys initial anxieties. If we refuse to accept the suggestions of the material imagination, if we do not understand that, for an active material imagination, *silent air* is silence actualized in a primal element, we refuse the tonality of images; we transcribed in the abstract the experiences of concrete imagination. How could we then experience a beneficial organic influence from reading Nietzsche? Nietzsche warns his readers in *Ecce Homo*:

> He who knows how to breathe in the air of my writings is aware that it is the air of the heights, that it is invigorating. A man must be built for it, or he runs the risk that it will chill him. The ice is near, the loneliness is terrible – but how serenely everything lies in the sunshine! How freely one can breathe! How much one feels lies beneath one! [26]

Cold, silence, height – three roots of a single substance. To cut one of them is to destroy Nietzschean life. For example, a cold silence must be haughty. For lack of this third root it is but a withdrawn, sullen, earthly silence that does not *breathe*, that does not penetrate the chest like the air of the heights. Similarly, for Nietzsche, a howling north wind would be nothing but a beast to be mastered, *to be silenced*. The cold wind of the heights is a dynamic being, it neither howls nor murmurs: it is silent. Finally, if a warm air tried to teach us silence, it would lack aggressiveness. Silence needs the aggressiveness of cold. As we can see, the triple correspondence is disturbed when we take away one attribute. But these negative proofs are artificial, and if we are willing to live in Nietzschean air, we will have innumerable positive proofs of the *correspondence* I am indicating. This correspondence brings out the contrasting correspondence of softness, music, and light through which Shelley's imagination breathes. As I have often said, the types of material imagination, however decisive they may be, do not efface the individual mark of genius. Shelley and Nietzsche are two geniuses who, in the same aerial homeland, worshiped opposing gods.

---

26 [Nietzsche,] *Poésies, Ecce Homo*, p. 13. [*Ecce Homo*, in *Gesammelte Werke*, vol. XXI, p. 298.]

Since I have devoted many pages in this work to the *dream of flight* – aerial sleep – I shall examine somewhat more closely a passage in Nietzsche that shows quite evidently *winged oneiric life* ...

Indeed, we cannot avoid seeing *a dream of flight* in the first paragraph of "On the Three Evils." "In a dream – in the last dream of the morning, I stood in the foothills today – beyond the world, held scales, and weighed the world." [27]

A reader distorted by intellectualism who places abstract thoughts before metaphor, who thinks that writing is looking for images in order to straight thoughts, will certainly object that this weighing of the world – he will doubtless prefer to say this ponderal evaluation – is only a metaphor expressing an evaluation of the *moral world*. But it would be most interesting to study this shift from the moral to the physical world. Any moralist should at least pose the problem of the *verbal expression* of moral facts. A thesis such as mine, treating imagination is a fundamental psychic value, poses this problem in the opposite sense: it examines how images of elevation prepare the dynamics of moral life. And in my opinion, Nietzsche's poetics plays precisely this precursory role: it paves the way for Nietzsche's ethics. But I do not wish to enter into this polemic. I prefer to stay within the limits of a study of the imaginary and just to ask my adversaries a polemic question on the psychological level: in a dream, in a morning dream, why see oneself atop a promontory? Instead of describing the panorama of a world in the first place to see the dreamer so easily enter a weigher's dream? But let us read a little further: "Weighable by a good weigher, reachable by strong wings: ... thus my dream found the world." [28] How can we explain, by other principles than those of ascensional psychology, that the dream that *weighs* the world is at the same time the one whose *vigorous wings* are going to overcome weight? The weigher of the world immediately, suddenly, enjoys a winged lightness.

27   [Nietzsche,] *Ainsi parlait Zarathoustra*, p. 262. [*Thus Spoke Zarathustra*, in *The Portable Nietzsche*, p. 298.]
28   [Nietzsche,] *Ainsi parlait Zarathoustra*, p. 263. [*Thus Spoke Zarathustra*, in *The Portable Nietzsche*, p. 299.]

We must therefore see that the true filiation of images works in the reverse order: it is because he has winged lightness that *weighs* the world ...

In the chapter "The Spirit of Heavens," Nietzsche says, "He who will one day teach men to fly will have moved all boundary stones; the boundary stones themselves will fly up into the air before him, and he will re-baptize the earth – 'the light one.'" [29] As George Meredith also writes: "Barriers are for those who do not know how to fly."

For the *material imagination*, flight is not a mechanism to be invented, it is matter to be transmuted, it is the fundamental basis for a transmutation of all values. Our being must lose its *earthliness* and become *aerial*. Then, it will make all earth *light*. Our own earth, within us, will be "the light one."

One might be tempted to explain this lyricism of the heights by reference to the reality of mountain life. One could recall Nietzsche's long stay at Sils Maria, noting that it was there, in 1881, that the idea of Zarathustra came to him "6,000 feet above sea level and even higher above all human things." One might also note that the "decisive part" of the third book of *Zarathustra*, "On Old and New Tables," "was composed during the arduous climb from the station to Eze, the wonderful Moorish village in the rocks ... beneath the Halcyon sky of Nice," [30] in a remarkably luminous winter.

But such a realism does not have the explanatory force one might grant it. Nietzsche does not seem in reality to have climbed to the peaks where "the chamois itself has lost its trail." Nietzsche was not a mountain climber. On the whole, he haunted high plateaus more than peaks. His poems were often composed upon his *descent* from the heights, upon his return to the valleys where men live.

But the *imaginary climate* is more important than the real one. Nietzsche's imagination is more instructive than any experience. It produces a climate of imaginary altitude and leads us into a special lyrical universe. The first transmutation of Nietzschean values is a transmutation of images. It transforms the richness of depth into a

29 [*Thus Spoke Zarathustra*, in *The Portable Nietzsche*, p. 304.]
30 [*Ecce Homo*, in *Gesammelte Werke*, vol. XXI, p. 253.]

glory of the heights. Nietzsche seeks to go beyond the depths, beyond evil, and beyond the heights, that is to say, beyond the noble,
for he is not satisfied with a tradition of prestige. He stretches all
moral forces between these imaginary poles, rejecting any utilitarian
material *progress* that would be merely horizontal, without a modi-
fication of our heavy being. Nietzsche devotes all his lyrical energy
to a change from heavy to light, from the terrestrial to the aerial. He
gives to the abyss the language of the summits. The cave suddenly
gives off aerial echoes: "Hail to me ... my abyss speaks, I have turned
my ultimate depth inside out into the light!" [31] Some might insist
on speaking of symbol, allegory, metaphor, and ask the philosopher
to designate moral lessons before images. But if images were not an
integral part of moral thought, they would not have such life, such
continuity. Nietzscheanism is for me a Manichaeanism of the imagination. It is tonic and beneficent because it stimulates our dynamic
being with the most active images. If my thesis is well-founded, we
ought to be able to discover a double perspective of height and of
depth in actions that truly engage one's entire being.

Matter and Subjective Depth

TR: 50–52

If we examine C.G. Jung's long study of alchemy, we can take fuller
measure of the dream of the depth of substances. Indeed, as Jung
demonstrated, the alchemist *projects* on patiently worked substances his own unconscious, which accompanies and parallels sensory
knowledge. If the alchemist speaks of mercury, he is thinking *exter-
nally* of quicksilver, yet at the same time, he believes himself to be
in the presence of a hidden spirit, imprisoned in the matter; [32] but
within this term of *spirit*, to which Cartesian physics will give reality,

---

31 "Le Convalescent," [Nietzsche,] *Ainsi parlait Zarathoustra*, p. 306. [*Thus
Spoke Zarathustra*, in *The Portable Nietzsche*, p. 328.]
32 See C.G. Jung, *Psychologie und Alchemie* [Zurich: Rascher Verlag, 1944],
p. 399. [*Psychology and Alchemy*, in *Collected Works of C.G. Jung*, vol. 12, trans.
R.F.C. Hull, (Princeton, N.J.: Princeton University Press, 1953–79).]

an undefined dream is beginning to work – a thought that cannot be enclosed within definitions, that multiplies meanings and words in order not to be imprisoned in precise meanings. Even though Jung warns us against assuming the unconscious to be located beneath consciousness, it seems to me that we can say the alchemist's unconscious projects itself into material images as a *depth*. In short, I shall say that the alchemist *projects his depth*. In several of the following chapters, I shall explore this same projection. So I shall come back to this discussion. Bu I think it useful to point out, at every opportunity, a law that I shall call the isomorphism of depth images. Dreaming depth, we dream *our* depth. Dreaming of the secret power of substances, we dream of our secret being. But the greatest secrets of our being are hidden from ourselves, they are hidden in our depths.

A complete study of the material images of the inner depths should consider at length all the values of hidden warmth. Should I undertake it, I would have to reconsider my entire work on fire, emphasizing some aspects that make it possible to speak of a true dialectics of warmth and fire. When warmth and fire take on their distinct images, it seems that these can be used to designate an introverted and an extroverted imagination. Fire exteriorizes itself, explodes, reveals itself. Warmth interiorizes itself, concentrates, hides itself. Warmth, rather than fire, deserves the name of the *third dimension*, according to the dreamlike metaphysics of Schelling: "Fire is nothing but pure substance – or the third dimension breaking through corporeality." [33]

The dream interior is warm, never burning. Dream warmth is always gentle, constant, regular. Through warmth, everything is *deep*. Warmth is the sign of a depth, the sense of a depth.

33   [Friedrich Wilhelm Joseph von Schelling, *Werke*, vol. I (Leipzig: Fritz Eckardt Verlag, 1907), p. 178.]

A Psychological Reading of Poe's "Narrative of Arthur Gordon Pym"

ER: 81–86

... I (re)placed "Pym" among the great works of Edgar Allan Poe. [34] Working on this example I understood with particular clarity the value of the *new methods of reading* provided by the *totality* of the new psychological schools. As soon as one reads a work with these new methods of analysis in mind, one participates in extremely diverse sublimations that incorporate remote images and that give wings to the imagination in multiple ways. Classical literary criticism impedes these divergent flights. In its pretensions to an instinctive psychological knowledge, to a native psychological intuition that is not acquired, it refers literary works to an outdated and hackneyed psychological experience, to a *closed experience*. It simply forgets the poetic function of giving a new form to the world that does not exist poetically if it is not ceaselessly re-imagined.

Here is the astonishing passage in which no voyager, no geographer, no realist will recognize a terrestrial water. The location of the island on which this extraordinary water is found, according to the narrator, is "83° 20' latitude, 43° 5' west longitude." This water is used as drink by all the savages of the island. We will see if it can satisfy thirst, if it can, like the water of the great poem "Annabel Lee," "quench all thirst": [35]

> On account of the singular character of the water, we refused to taste it, supposing it to be polluted; and it was not until some time afterwards we came to understand that such was the appearance of the streams throughout the whole group. I am at a loss to give a distinct idea of the nature of this liquid, and cannot do so without many words. Although it flowed with rapidity in all declivities where common water would do so, yet never, except when falling in a cascade, had it the customary appearance

---

34 [In the preceding paragraph Bachelard has confessed that at first he was bored by this narrative loaded with apparently absurd technical details.]

35 [The phrase comes, in fact, from lines 37–38 of the poem "For Annie." Here, Bachelard is obviously quoting from memory, as he often does.]

of limpidity. It was, nevertheless, in point of fact, as perfectly limpid as any limestone water in existence, the difference being only in appearance. At first sight, and especially in cases where little declivity was found, it bore resemblance, as regards consistency, to a thick infusion of gum Arabic in common water. But this was only the least remarkable of its extraordinary qualities. It was not colourless nor was it of any uniform colour – presenting to the eye as it flowed every possible shade of purple, like the hues of a changeable silk ... Upon collecting a basinful and allowing it to settle thoroughly, we perceived that the whole mass of liquid was made up of a number of distinct veins, each of a distinct hue; that these veins did not commingle; that their cohesion was perfect in regard to their own particles among themselves, and imperfect in regard to neighbouring veins. Upon passing the blade of a knife athwart the veins, the water closed over it immediately, as with us, and also, in withdrawing it, all traces of the passage of the knife were instantly obliterated. If, however, the blade was passed down accurately between two veins, a perfect separation was effected, which the power of cohesion did not immediately rectify. The phenomena of this water formed the first definite link in that vast chain of apparent miracles with which I was destined to be at length encircled. [36]

Marie Bonaparte has not overlooked these two extraordinary pages. She cites them in her book after resolving the question of the dominant phantasms that guide the narrator. She therefore simply adds:

This "water," as we shall have no difficulty in recognizing, represents blood. We are expressly told that it flowed in "veins," while the land that differed "essentially from any hitherto visited by civilized man," a land in which there was nothing with which they were formerly conversant, is, on the contrary, that with which we are all conversant; namely, the body on whose blood we fed long before we were nourished by its milk: that of the mother in whose

---

36 Edgar Allan Poe, *Aventures d'Arthur Gordon Pym*, trans. Charles Baudelaire [Paris: Lévy, 1858], pp. 210–11. ["Narrative of A. Gordon Pym," in *The Complete Works of Edgar Allan Poe*, vol. III, ed. James A. Harrison (New York: AMS Press, 1965), pp. 186–87.]

> womb we were borne. Here the reader is expected to object
> that our interpretations are monotonous in their repeti-
> tion and alway revert to the same themes. The fault, how-
> ever, is not ours but rather that of the human unconscious
> that, from its prehistoric past, draws up a few eternal
> themes on which to weave its innumerable variations.
> It need not, therefore, surprise us that the same basic
> themes re-emerge through the elaborated surfaces of
> these variations. [37]

I have a reason for quoting this psychoanalytical explanation in detail. It provides a shining example of the *organic materialism* that is so
active in the unconscious, as I have indicated in my introduction. The
reader who has studied Marie Bonaparte's great work page by page
has no doubt that the hemoptyses that led first to the death of Poe's
mother, and subsequently to the deaths of all the women he loved
faithfully, left a lifelong mark on the poet's unconscious. Poe himself
wrote: "And 'blood,' too, that word of all words – so rife at all times
with mystery, and suffering, and terror – how trebly full of import
did it now appear – how chillily and heavily (disjointed, as it thus
was, from any foregoing words to qualify or render it distinct) did
its vague syllables fall, amid the deep gloom of my prison, into the
innermost recesses of my soul!" [38] Thus we can see why everything
in nature that flows heavily, painfully, mysteriously, might be, for so
strongly marked a psyche, like an accursed blood that carries death
in its current. When a liquid assumes a value, it becomes related to
an organic liquid. There is therefore a poetics of blood. It is a poetics
of tragedy and pain, for blood is never happy.

However, there is room for a poetics of *valorous* blood. Paul
Claudel gives this poetics of *living blood* a kind of life that is quite different from that found in Poe's poetry. Here is an example in which
blood is a water valorized in this manner: "Any water is desirable to
us; and certainly, more than the blue and virgin sea, this one appeals

---

37   Marie Bonaparte, *Edgar Poe: Étude psychanalytique* [Paris: Éditions Denöel
et Steele, 1933], p. 418. [*The Life and Works of Edgar Allan Poe*, trans. John Rodker
(London: Imago Publishing Co., 1949), p. 332.]
38   Poe, *Aventures d'Arthur Gordon Pym*, p. 47. ["Narrative of A. Gordon Pym," p,
41.]

to what there is in us between the flesh and the soul: our human water charged with force and spirit, the burning, dark blood." [39]

With Gordon Pym we are apparently at the opposite pole of inner life: adventures have to be geographical. But the narrator who
starts with a descriptive tale feels the need to give an impression
of strangeness. He must therefore invent; he must draw on his unconscious. Why could not water, that universal liquid, also take on a
singular property? Discovered water will thus be an invented liquid.
Invention, governed by the laws of the unconscious, suggests an organic liquid. It could be milk. But Poe's unconscious bears a particular, a fatal mark: valorization will be accomplished through blood.
Here the consciousness intervenes: the word is not to be written on
that page. Even if the word were to be pronounced, everything would
rise up against it: consciousness would repress it, logically as an
absurdity, experimentally as an impossibility, personally as an accursed memory. The extraordinary water that astonishes the traveler
will then be an unnamed blood, an unnameable blood. So much for
the analysis regarding the author.

As for the reader, either his unconscious already has the valorization of blood – although this is far from being the general case – and
the page is readable: with the proper orientation, it can even move
him; it may also displease and even repel him, thereby demonstrating the existence of valorization. Or else the reader lacks this valorization of liquid by blood: the page loses all its significance; it is
incomprehensible. When I first read it during my positivist period I
saw in it only a too facile and arbitrary invention. Since then, I have
understood that if this passage has no objective truth, it has at least a
subjective meaning. This subjective meaning compels the attention of
the psychologist who takes the trouble to trace back the dreams that
precede the works.

However, classical psychoanalysis, whose lessons I followed in this
particular interpretation, does not seem to account for all the imagery. It neglects the study of the intermediary zone between blood and
water, between the unnameable and the named. It is precisely in this

39   Paul Claudel, Connaissance del'Est [Paris: Mercure de France, 1907], p. 105.

intermediary zone, where expression requires *many words*, that Poe's passage bears the mark of genuinely experienced liquids. It is not the unconscious that would suggest the experiment of slipping a knife between the veins of this extraordinary water. That requires a positive familiarity with *fibrillary* water, with a liquid that, although formless, has an internal structure and, as such, is a source of endless fascination to the material imagination. I believe it is possible therefore to assert that during his childhood Poe was interested in jellies and gums; seeing that, when a gum is thickened, it takes on a fibrous structure, he slipped a knife blade between the fibers. He says so, why not believe him? It is possible that he dreamed of blood while kneading the gum, but it is because he did this – as many others have done – that he did not hesitate to put into a *realistic* narrative rivers that flow slowly, that in flowing maintain veins like thickened water. In accordance with the previously mentioned law of the active imagination, Poe transposed limited experiences to a cosmic level. In the storehouses in which he played as a child, there was molasses. That too was a *melancholy* matter. One hesitates to taste it, especially when one has a strict foster father like John Allan. But what a pleasure it is to stir it with a wooden spoon! What a joy as well to pull and cut the marshmallow paste! The natural chemistry of familiar materials gives its first lesson to dreamers who do not hesitate to write cosmological poems. The heavy water of Poe's metapoetics obviously has a *component* drawn from a very childish physics. I had to point this out before coming back to an examination of more human, more dramatic *components*.

The Insufficiency of Perception

ER: 162–64

... It might seem that the affirmation of this immediate adherence to a maternal image poses incorrectly the problem of image and metaphor. [40] To contradict me, one might argue that vision itself, the

40 [In the preceding passage, Bachelard has analyzed images of water (particularly from *La Mer* by Jules Michelet) that impart a maternal character to an entire landscape.]

mere contemplation of spectacles of nature, also seems to impose images directly. One could point out, for instance, that a great number of poets, inspired by a serene vision, tell us of the milky beauty of a peaceful moonlit lake. Let us discuss then this image that is so common to the poetry of water. Although it appears to be very unfavorable to my thesis concerning the material imagination, the image will finally prove that the attraction it exerts upon the most diverse poets can be explained by matter and not by forms or colors.

How in fact can the reality of this image be physically represented? In other words, what are the objective conditions that determine the creation of this particular image?

In order for the milky image to come to the imagination in the presence of a tranquil lake beneath the moon, the lunar light must be diffused – the water must be agitated very slightly, and yet agitated enough so that the surface does not reflect crudely the landscape lighted by the moonbeams – in sum, the water must go from transparence to translucence, it must slowly become opaque, it must become opaline. But that is all it can do. And is it really enough to make one think of a bowl of milk, of the milkmaid's foamy bucket, of real milk? It does not seem so. We must therefore admit that neither the principle nor the force of the image is to be found in visual data. To justify the poet's conviction, to justify the frequency and naturalness of the image, we must include in it components that are not *seen*, whose nature is not *visual*. These are precisely the components through which material imagination will be manifested ...

What then is the basis of this image of milky water? It is the image of a warm and happy night, the image of a clear and enveloping matter. An image that includes air and water, sky and earth, and unites them: a cosmic image, broad, immense, and soft. If we really experience this, we recognize that it is not the world that is bathed in the milky light of the moon but rather the spectator who is bathed in so physical and so sure a delight that it recalls the most ancient well-being, the sweetest of foods. That is why the milk of the river will never be icy. Never will the poet say that the winter moon pours a milky light on the waters. The mildness of the air, the softness of the light, the serenity of the soul are essential to the image. These are its material components, its strong and primordial components. *Whiteness only comes afterwards.* It is deduced. It comes as an adjective evoked by the substantive and after the substantive. In the realm of dreams, the word order that says that a color is white as milk is misleading. The dreamer first apprehends the milk, then his drowsy eye *sometimes* sees its whiteness.

We will not quibble over whiteness in the realm of images. Were a golden moonbeam added to the river, the formal and superficial imagination of colors would not be disturbed. Surface imagination will see what is yellow as white because the material image of milk is sufficiently intense to continue its gentle progression deep within the human heart, *to actualize* completely the calm of the dreamer, to provide a matter, a substance, for an impression of happiness. Milk is the first of sedatives. The calm of man thus imbues the contemplated waters with milk. In *Éloges* St. John Perse writes:

> ... Now these calm waters are of milk, and all things overflowing in the soft solitudes of morning. [41]

A foaming torrent, however white, can never have such a privilege. Thus, color is really nothing when the material imagination dreams of its primal elements.

The Complex of Novalis

ER: 174–75

This valorization of substance that makes of water an inexhaustible milk, the milk of mother nature, is not the only one that endows water with a profoundly feminine character. In the life of every man, or at least in the dream life of every man, appears the second woman: mistress or wife. The second woman will also be projected upon nature. The wife-mistress landscape takes its place beside the mother landscape. Of course, these natures may interfere or mask each other, but there are cases in which they may be distinguished. I shall give

---

41 [St. John Perse, *Éloges and Other Poems*, trans. Louise Varèse (New York: W.W. Norton and Co., 1944), p. 62.]

an example in which the projection of the wife nature is very clear. Indeed, one of Novalis's dreams will provide us with further reasons to assert the feminine substantiality of water.

After dipping his hands and moistening his lips in a pool he happens upon in his dream, Novalis is seized by "an irresistible desire to bathe in it." No *vision* invites him to do so. It is the very *substance* he has touched with his hands and lips that summons him. It summons him materially, by virtue of what seems to be a magical participation.

The dreamer undresses and enters the pool. Only at this moment do the images appear: they emerge from matter, they arise, as if from a seed, out of a primitive sensual reality, a rapture that cannot yet project itself:

> From all sides, there sprang forth unknown images, which melted one into the other, becoming visible beings and surrounding the dreamer, so that each wave of the delicious element clung to him tightly like a sweet breast. It was as if a group of lovely girls had dissolved in this water, and for an instant became bodies again at the contact of the young man. [42]

In this marvelous text, which demonstrates a profoundly materialized imagination, water – in its volume, in its mass, and no longer in the mere enchantment of its reflections – appears as *dissolved girl*, [43] as a liquid *essence of girl*, "eine Auflösung reizender Mädchen."

Feminine forms will rise out of the very substance of water, at the contact of the man's breast, apparently when the man's desire take a precise form. But the *voluptuous substance* exists before the forms of voluptuousness ...

... Novalis's visions do not seem to be active ones. The lovely young girls quickly dissolve again into the element, and the dreamer, "transported with delight," continues his journey with out having any further experience with the ephemeral girls.

42 Novalis, *Henri d'Ofterdingen*, [trans. G. Polti and P. Morisse (Paris: Mercure de France, 1908,] p. 9. [*Heinrich von Ofterdingen* (Leipzig: Edda-Verlag, 1924), p. 10.]
43 [In French: "L'eau ... apparait comme de la jeune fille dissoute." Bachelard uses the partitive *de la* instead of the more common indefinite article *une* to emphasize the material assimilation of girl and *water*.]

Thus the dream beings in Novalis exist only when one touches them; water becomes woman only against the breast: it does not provide distant images. This very strange physical character of some of Novalis's dreams seems to call for a name. Instead of saying that Novalis is a *seer* who sees the invisible, we would readily say that he is a *toucher* who touches the untouchable, the impalpable, the unreal. He goes deeper than any other dreamer. His dream is a dream within a dream, not in the ethereal sense but in the sense of depth ...

As I have already indicated in my *Psychoanalyse du feu*, Novalis's imagination is directed by a *caloricity*, that is, by the desire for a warm, soft, enveloping, protective substance, by the need of a matter that surrounds the entire being and permeates it. It is an imagination that develops in depth. The phantoms emerge from the substance as vaporous but full forms, as beings that, although ephemeral, one has been able to touch, and to which one has transmitted a little of the deep warmth of inner life. All of Novalis's dreams bear the seal of this depth. The dream in which he finds this marvelous water, this water that places girl everywhere, which offers girl in the *partitive*, is not a dream with a wide horizon, with a broad vision. It is in the depth of a cave, down in the earth, that he finds the wonderful lake that jealously guards its sweet warmth. Moreover, the visual images that arise from a water so deeply charged with value will have no consistency; they will melt into each other, retaining thus the hydrous and calorific mark of their origin. Matter alone will remain. For such an imagination, everything disappears in the realm of the formal image, nothing disappears in the realm of the material image. The phantoms that truly arise from substance do not need further involvement in a precise activity. Even though the water clings "like a sweet breast" to the dreamer, he will not ask for anything more. For he enjoys substantial possession. How could he help feeling a sort of disdain for forms? Forms are a kind of clothing; a too well delineated nudity is icy, closed, enclosed within its lines. Consequently, for one whose dreams are marked by warmth, the imagination is purely a *material imagination*. It is of matter that he dreams, its warmth that he needs. Of what importance are fleeting visions when, in the secret of night, in the solitude of a shadowy cave, one holds reality in its essence, with its weight, its substantial life! ...

Novalis's dreams go so deep that they may seem exceptional. Nevertheless we might perceive their faint outline in certain meta-phors, if we search a little beneath formal images. For instance, in a line of Ernest Renan we may recognize the traces of Novalis's phan-tom. In his *Studies of Religious History*, Renan discusses the epithet given to the river, *kalli-parthenoi* (beautiful maidens), and says calmly that its waves "turned into girls." [44] Even if we examine the image from every possible angle, we will find *no formal character*. There is no linear pattern to justify it. We defy any psychologist of the imagina-tion of forms to explain this image. It can only be explained by the material imagination. The water is given its whiteness and limpid-ity by an internal matter. This matter is *dissolved girl*. The water has taken on the property of the dissolved feminine substance. If you want immaculate water, dissolve virgins in it. If you want the seas of Melanesia, dissolve Negresses in it.

Oneiric Flight: The Insufficiency of Psychoanalysis in Aesthetics

---

AS: 27–29

Classical psychoanalysis has often treated its knowledge of *symbols* as if symbols were concepts. We might even say that symbols are the fundamental concepts of psychoanalytical investigation. Once a symbol has been interpreted, once it has been given its *unconscious meaning*, it becomes merely an instrument for analysis and does not seem to require further study in its context and in its varieties. In this way, for classical psychoanalysis, the dream of flight has become one of the clearest symbols, one of the most common *explanatory concepts*: it symbolizes, we are told, sensual desires. Through it, innocent con-fessions are immediately stigmatized: it seems to be an unmistak-able sign. Since the dream of flight is particularly clear and striking, and since its confession, seemingly quite innocent, is not hindered by any censorship, it is often one of the first experiences interpreted

44 [Ernest Renan, *Études d'histoire religieuse* (Paris: Calmann Lévy, 1897), p. 32.]

in the analysis of dreams. It illuminates in a flash an entire oneiric situation.[45]

Such a method, which gives once and for all a definite meaning to a particular symbol, disregards many problems. It disregards particularly the problem of imagination, as if imagination were the futile distraction of a persistent emotional preoccupation. Classical psychoanalysis lacks the requisite curiosity in at least two respects: it does not account for the *aesthetic* character of the dream flight; and it does not account for the efforts toward rationalization that shape and deform this fundamental dream.

Even if we admit, along with psychoanalysis, that *oneiric sensuality* is satisfied by having the dreamer fly, how is this secret, obscure, indistinct impression going to take on the *graceful* images of flight? How, in its fundamental monotony, is it to become so cloaked in picturesqueness as to give rise to endless accounts of winged voyages?

The answers to these two questions, which appear so specialized, would constitute a contribution to the aesthetics of love and to a rationalization of imaginary voyages as well.

The first question gives a new point of view on the aesthetics of gracefulness. Visual description does not say all there is to say about this aesthetics. Every Bergsonian knows that a gracefully curved trajectory must be traced with a sympathetic inner movement. Every graceful line thus reveals a kind of *linear hypothesis*: it leads our reverie by giving it the continuity of a line. But beyond this imitative intuition that obeys, there is always an impulse that commands. Dynamic imagination suggests, to one who contemplates a graceful line, the wildest substitution: it is you, dreamer, who are the evolving grace. Feel in yourself the *force of gracefulness.* Realize that you are a reserve of gracefulness, a potentiality of flight. Understand that you hold, within your very will, curled volutes, like the young fern leaf.

---

45 Of course, psychoanalytic practice contributes many nuances that complicate symbolization. For instance, in reference to *dreams of stairways,* often so close to dreams of flight, Dr. René Allendy remarks: "Men climb steps (activity) and women descend (passivity)." *Rêves expliqués* [Paris: Gallimard, 1938], p. 176. In addition, Allendy indicates numerous inversions that diversify this very simple dream.

With whom, for whom, against whom are you graceful? Is your flight a deliverance or is it an abduction? Do you take pleasure in your goodness or in your strength? In your skill or in your nature? In flight, sensuality is *beautiful*. The dream of flight is the dream of a *seductive charmer*. Love and its images build upon this theme. By studying it we shall thus see how love *produces* images.

To answer the second question, we must consider the readiness with which the dream of flight is rationalized. During the span of the dream itself, this flight is tirelessly commented upon by the dreamer's intelligence; it is explained by long speeches that the dreamer addresses to himself. The flier, within his very dream, declares himself the inventor of his flight. There is thus formed in the dreamer's mind a clear awareness of himself as a flying man. This is a marvelous example for studying, within the dream, the logical and objective construction of dream images. If we follow a dream as well-defined as the dream of flight, we realize that a dream can be logical in its ideas just as much as it can be stubbornly emotional in its amorous passion.

Psychoanalysis does not say everything when it asserts the erotic character of oneiric flight. Oneiric flight, like all psychological symbols, requires a multiple interpretation: an interpretation through passion, an aesthetically oriented interpretation, and a rational and objective interpretation.

The Psychology of Resistance

TV: 19–21

Psychoanalysts will immediately raise an objection: they will say that the real adversaries are human, that the child encounters his first restrictions in the family, and that, in general, the *resistances* that daunt the psyche are of a social nature. [46] But if we limit ourselves, as psychoanalysis often does, to translating symbols into human terms, we

---

46 [Bachelard is aware of the possibility that psychoanalysts may criticize the idea that imagination of resistance is born in the confrontation with material objects.]

neglect an entire field of study – the autonomy of symbolism – which is precisely what I want to bring to the reader's attention. If, in the world of symbols, resistance is human, in the world of energy it is material. Psychoanalysis has been no more able than psychology to find proper means of estimating these forces. It lacks the psychical dynamometer that active work with matter provides. Like descriptive psychology, it is limited to a sort of psychical topology: it defines various levels, strata, associations, complexes, symbols. It is true that psychoanalysis evaluates dominant impulses by their results. But it has not prepared the means for a true *psychical dynamics*, a precise dynamics investigating the individuality of images. In other words, psychoanalysis merely defines images by their symbolism. As soon as an instinctual image has been detected or a traumatic memory brought to light, psychoanalysis raises the question of *social* interpretation. It neglects an entire domain of research: the very domain of the imagination, whereas the psyche is animated *by* a veritable *hunger for images*. It wants images. In sum, under the image, psychoanalysis seeks reality; it ignores the inverse investigation that starts from reality in order to seek the positive character of the image. It is in this research that we detect that imaginative energy that is the very mark of the active psyche.

Too often the psychoanalyst considers storytelling as if it were hiding something. It is a cover, and therefore performs secondary function. But, as soon as the hand takes part in storytelling, as soon as real energies are engaged in a work, as soon as the imagination actualizes its images, the substance of unhappiness dissolves. Action is therefore the negation of unhappiness. The problem, then, is the maintenance of a dynamic state, the restoration of dynamic will, through the rhythmanalysis [47] of aggressiveness and mastery. Image is always an enhancement of being. Imagination and stimulation are linked.

47   [From the neologism *rythmanalyse*, which for Bachelard refers to a psychotherapy based on an understanding of human biological and psychological rhythms. In *La Dialectique de la durée* he develops his idea of a "vibrating" human time and devotes an entire chapter (pp. 147–70) to the work of a Brazilian philosopher, Lucio Alberto Pinheiro dos Santos, *Rhythmanalysis: Space, Time and Everyday Life* (London: Continuum, 2004).]

Of course, unfortunately, there are stimuli without images, but nevertheless there are no images without stimulation ...

What would a resistance be if it had no persistence, no substantive depth – the very depth of matter? Psychologists may insist that in an outburst of anger a child will hit the table he has bumped into; [48] but this *gesture*, this ephemeral rage releases the aggressiveness too quickly for us to find in it the true images of aggressive imagination. Later on we shall consider the imaginary inventions of discursive anger, the anger that stirs the worker against ever rebellious, primally rebellious matter. But we must understand right away that active imagination does not start as a simple reaction, as a reflex. Imagination needs a dialectical animism, one that is experienced when we isolate in the object its responses to intentional acts of violence, when we assign the initiative of provocation to the worker. Imagination that is material and dynamic enables us to experience a provoked adversity, a psychology of *opposition* [49] that does not settle for the blow, the shock, but that seeks domination over the very heart of matter. Therefore the dreamed hardness is a hardness repeatedly attacked, which constantly repeats its stimulation. If we take hardness as the mere motive for an exclusion, in its initial *no*, we dream in its external, its intangible form. For the dreamer of inner hardness, granite is a type of provocation; its hardness offends, in a way that cannot be avenged without arms, tools, without the means of human guile. One does not treat granite with childish anger. It must be scored or polished in a new dialectic in which the dynamics of *opposition* may find the opportunity for nuances.

48   Is this really a natural experience? How many parents teach this childish vengeance themselves to their little ones!
49   [Here Bachelard uses the preposition *against* as a noun in the expression: "Une psychologie du contre."]

The Poetic Significance of Reverie

PR: 9–11

Psychology has more to lose than to gain by allowing etymological derivations to inspire the formation of its basic notions. [50] Etymology softens the sharpest distinctions that separate dream and reverie. Furthermore, since psychologists are anxious to find what is most typical, they first study that fascinating nocturnal dream and they give little attention to reveries, which are for them but confused, structureless dreams, without narrative content or enigmas. Reverie then appears as a bit of nocturnal matter left behind in the brightness of day. If the oneiric matter condenses a little in the dreamer's soul, then the reverie falls into dream, and the "puffs of reverie" noted by psychiatrists stifle the psyche; reverie becomes somnolence, and the dreamer falls into sleep. In the continuity from reverie to dream, there is thus a sort of fatality of the fall. What a poor reverie if it only leads to the siesta! We must even wonder whether the unconscious itself does not suffer a decline of being in this *going-to-sleep*. The unconscious will recover its activity in the dreams of true sleep. And psychology works toward the two poles of clear thought and nocturnal dream, assured in this way of embracing in its examination the entire domain of the human psyche.

But there are other reveries that do not belong to this twilight state in which diurnal life and nocturnal life are blended. For many reasons, diurnal reverie deserves direct study. Reverie is too normal a spiritual phenomenon – and too useful, as well, to psychic balance – to be treated as a derivative of the dream, to be classified without discussion among the oneiric phenomena. In short, it is appropriate, in determining the essence of reverie, to return to reverie itself. And it is precisely through phenomenology that the distinction between

---

50 [Bachelard is referring here to the etymological connection between the French words for dream (*rêve*) and reverie (*rêverie*).]

dream and reverie can be clarified, since a possible intervention of consciousness provides a decisive sign.

We may wonder whether there really exists a consciousness in dreams. A dream can have such a strange quality that it seems as if another subject has come to dream in us: "I was visited by a dream." There we have the formula that stamps the passivity of great nocturnal dreams. We must take up residence in these dreams again to be convinced they were once ours. Afterward, we turn them into stories, into fables of a former time, adventures of another world. Tales of far-off lands are often embroidered en route. We often add, innocently, unconsciously, a detail to increase the picturesqueness of our venture into the realm of night. Have you ever noticed the expression of a man recounting his dream? He smiles at his involvement in its drama, at his fright. He is amused. He would like you to be amused too. [51] The dream-teller sometimes enjoys his dream as if it were an original work. He experiences in it a vicarious originality, so he is very surprised when a psychoanalyst tells him that another dreamer has experienced the same "originality." We should not be misled by the dreamer's conviction of having lived the dream that he is telling. It is an extrinsic conviction that is reinforced every time the story is told. There is certainly no similarity between the subject who narrates and the subject who dreamed. A truly phenomenological elucidation of nocturnal dreams is therefore a difficult problem. Undoubtedly, we would have a way to resolve this problem if we were to develop further a psychology, and subsequently a phenomenology, of reverie.

Instead of looking for dream in reverie, we would look for reverie in dream. There are areas of tranquility in the midst of nightmares. Robert Desnos has noted these interferences of dream and reverie: "Though asleep and dreaming, unable to separate exactly dream and

---

51 Often, I must admit, the teller of dreams bores me. If it were frankly reworked, perhaps his dream might interest me. But to listen to a glorified account of its insanity! I have not yet cleared up, psychoanalytically, this boredom on the account of another's dreams. Perhaps I still have some of the rationalist's inflexibility. I cannot docilely follow a boastfully incoherent narration. I always suspect a part of the reported nonsense of being invented nonsense.

reverie, I remain aware of decor." [52] This amounts to saying that the dreamer, in the darkness of sleep, finds the splendor of the day. Then he is conscious of the beauty of the world. For an instant, the beauty of the dreamed world restores his consciousness.

It is thus that reverie demonstrates repose of the being, that reverie illustrates a state of well-being.

The Phenomenological Approach

PE: 1–2, 12–13

When I shall have occasion to mention the relation of a new poetic image to an archetype lying dormant in the depths of the unconscious, I shall have to make it understood that this relation is not, properly speaking, a *causal* one. The poetic image is not subject to an inner thrust. It is not an echo of the past. On the contrary: through the brilliance of an image, the distant past resounds with echoes, and it is hard to know at what depth these echoes will reverberate and die away. Because of its novelty and its action, the poetic image has an entity and a dynamism of its own; it is refer able to a direct *ontology*. This ontology is what I plan to study. Very often, then, it is in the opposite of causality, that is, in *reverberation*, which has been so subtly analyzed by Minkowski, [53] that I think we find the real measure of

---

52 Robert Desnos, *Domaine public* (Paris: Gallimard, 1953), p. 348.
53 Cf. Eugène Minkowski, *Vers une cosmologie: Fragments philosophiques* (Paris: Aubier, 1936), chapter IX.

[Editor's note by Maria Jolas: "Eugène Minkowski, a prominent phenomenologist whose studies extend both in the fields of psychology and philosophy, followed Bergson in accepting the notion of 'élan vital' as the dynamic origin of human life. Without the vital impulse, as conceived by Bergson, the human being is static and therefore moribund. Referring to Anna Teresa Tymieniecka's book *Phenomenology and Science*, we can say that for Minkowski, the essence of life is not 'a feeling of being, of existence' but a feeling of participation in a flowing onward, necessarily expressed in terms of time, and secondarily expressed in terms of space. In view of this, Minkowski's choice of what he calls an auditive metaphor, *retentir*, is very apt, for in sound both time and space are epitomized. To understand Bachelard's reference, the following excerpt from Minkowski's *Vers une cosmologie* might be helpful:

the being of a poetic image. In this reverberation, the poetic image will have a sonority of being. The poet speaks on the threshold of being. Therefore, in order to determine the being of an image, we shall have to experience its reverberation in the manner of Minkowski's phenomenology.

To say that the poetic image is independent of causality is to make a rather serious statement. But the causes cited by psychologists and psychoanalysts can never really explain the wholly unexpected nature of the new image, any more than they can explain the attraction it

---

'If, having fixed the original form in our mind's eye, we ask ourselves how that form comes alive and fills with life, we discover a new dynamic and vital category, a new property of the universe: reverberation (retentir). It is as though a well-spring existed in a sealed vase and its waves, repeatedly echoing against the sides of this vase, filled it with their sonority. Or again, it is as though the sound of a hunting horn, reverberating everywhere through its echo, made the tiniest leaf, the tiniest wisp of moss shudder in a common movement and transformed the whole forest, filling it to its limits, into a vibrating, sonorous world ... What is secondary in these images, or, in other terms, what makes these images only images for us, are the sonorous well-spring, the hunting horn, the sealed vase, the echo, the reflection of sonorous waves against the sides – in a word, all that belongs to the material and palpable world.

'Suppose these elements were missing: would really nothing living subsist? For my part, I believe that this is precisely where we should see the world come alive and, independent of any instrument, of any physical properties, fill up with penetrating deep waves that, although not sonorous in the sensory meaning of the word, are not, for this reason, less harmonious, resonant, melodic and capable of determining the whole tonality of life. And this life itself will reverberate to the most profound depths of its being, through contact with these waves, which are at once sonorous and silent ... Here to fill up and plenitude will have a completely different sense. It is not a material object that fills another by espousing the form that the other imposes. No, it is the dynamism of the sonorous life itself that by engulfing and appropriating everything it finds in its path, fills the slice of space, or better, the slice of the world that it assigns itself by its movement, making it reverberate, breathing into its own life. The word slice must not be taken in its geometrical sense. It is not a matter of decomposing the world virtually or actually into sonorous balls, nor of tracing the limits of the sphere determined by the waves emanating from a sonorous source. In fact, our examples, the scaled vase, the forest, because of the very fact that they fill up with sounds, form a sort of self-enclosed whole, a microcosm ...'"]

holds for a mind that is foreign to the process of its creation. The poet does not confer the past of his image upon me, and yet his image immediately takes root in me. The communicability of an unusual image is a fact of great ontological significance. We shall return to this question of communion through brief, isolated, rapid actions. Images excite us – afterwards – but they are not the phenomena of an excitement. In all psychological research, we can, of course, bear in mind psychoanalytical methods for determining the personality of a poet, and thus find a measure of the pressures – but above all of the oppressions – that a poet has been subjected to in the course of his life. But the poetic act itself, the sudden image, the flare-up of being in the imagination, are inaccessible to such investigations. In order to clarify the problem of the poetic image philosophically, we shall have to have recourse to a phenomenology of the imagination. By this should be understood a study of the phenomenon of the poetic image when it emerges into the consciousness as a direct product of the heart, soul and being of man, apprehended in his actuality.

The phenomenological situation with regard to psychoanalytical investigation will perhaps be more precisely stated if, in connection with poetic images, we are able to isolate a sphere of *pure sublimation*; of a sublimation that sublimates nothing, that is relieved of the burden of passion and freed from the pressure of desire. By thus giving to the poetic image at its peak an absolute of sublimation, I place heavy stakes on a simple nuance. It seems to me, however, that poetry gives abundant proof of this absolute sublimation, as will be seen frequently in the course of this work. When psychologists and psychoanalysts are furnished this proof, they cease to see anything in the poetic image but a simple game, a short-lived, totally vain game. Images, in particular, have no significance for them – neither from the standpoint of the passions, nor from that of psychology or psychoanalysis. It does not occur to them that the significance of such images is precisely a poetic significance. But poetry is there with its countless surging images, images through which the creative imagination comes to live in its own domain.

For a phenomenologist, the attempt to attribute antecedents to an image, when we are in the very existence of the image, is a sign of inveterate psychologism. On the contrary, let us take the poetic image in its being. For the poetic consciousness is so wholly absorbed by the image that appears on the language, above customary language; the language it speaks with the poetic image is so new that correlations between past and present can no longer be usefully considered. The examples I shall give of breaks in significance, sensation, and sentiment will oblige the reader to grant me that the poetic image is under the sign of a new being.

This new being is happy man.

Happy in speech, therefore unhappy in reality, will be the psychoanalyst's immediate objection. Sublimation, for him, is nothing but a vertical compensation, a flight upwards, exactly in the same way that compensation is a lateral flight. And right away, the psychoanalyst will abandon ontological investigation of the image, to dig into the past of man. He sees and points out the poet's secret sufferings. He explains the flower by the fertilizer.

The phenomenologist does not go that far. For him, the image is there, the word speaks, the word of the poet speaks to him. There is no need to have lived through the poet's sufferings in order to seize the felicity of speech offered by the poet – a felicity that dominates tragedy itself. Sublimation in poetry towers above the psychology of the mundanely unhappy soul. For it is a fact that poetry possesses a felicity of its own, however great the tragedy it may be called upon to illustrate.

Pure sublimation, as I see it, poses a serious problem of method for, needless to say, the phenomenologist cannot disregard the deep psychological reality of the processes of sublimation that have been so lengthily examined by psychoanalysis. His task is that of proceeding phenomenologically to images that have not been experienced and that life does not prepare but that the poet creates; of living what has not been lived, and being receptive to an overture of language. There exist a few poems, such as certain poems by Pierre-Jean Jouve, in which experiences of this kind may be found. Indeed, I know of no oeuvre that has been nourished on psychoanalytical meditation more than Jouve's. However, here and there, his poetry passes through flames of such intensity that we no longer need live at its original source. He himself has said: "Poetry constantly surpasses its origins, and because it suffers more deeply in ecstasy or in sorrow, it retains greater freedom." [54]

54 Pierre-Jean Jouve, En Miroir [Paris: Mercure de France, 1964], p. 109. Andrée Chédid has also written: "A poem remains free. We shall never enclose its fate in our own." The poet knows well that "his breath will carry him farther than his desire." Terre et poésie [Paris: Guy Levis Mano, 1956], pars. 14 and 25.

IV

THE ALCHEMY
OF IMAGINATION

[The texts presented in this section illustrate the co-
operation of the real and the unreal in the dynamics of images. Such a fusion restores to imagination
its anchorage in time and space. It shows how the
contradictions and inexactitudes of images can simultaneously astonish and convince the reader.
Indeed, Bachelard mixes examples drawn from real
life with passages of literary analyses. He does not
imply, however, that actual experience could explain
the content of images. We must never forget that the
poet "does not create the way he lives, he lives the
way he creates" (PE: 15). Better than common experiences, which are frozen by logical and utilitarian categories, poetry reveals an active contact with
the world; it enables us to discover a reality already
enchanted by imagination, already composed of
dynamic contraries. The alchemy of images has its
source in the inversion of the subject and the universe, in which Bachelard sees the "total metaphor"
(TR: 199). – Ed.]

Inversion of Vision and the Visible

ER: 40–42, 44–45

The philosophy of Schopenhauer has shown that aesthetic contemplation soothes for a moment the unhappiness of man by detaching him from the tragedy of will. This separation of contemplation from will does away with a characteristic that I would like
to emphasize: the will to contemplate. Contemplation, too, involves

a will. Man wants to see. Seeing is a direct need. Curiosity gives dynamism to the human mind. But in nature itself, there seem to be *forces of vision* at work. The relations between *contemplated nature* and *contemplative nature* are close and reciprocal. *Imaginary nature* achieves unity between *natura naturans* and *natura naturata*. When a poet lives his dream and his poetic creations, he achieves this natural unity. It seems then that contemplated nature aids contemplation, that it already contains some means of contemplation. The poet asks us "to associate with ourselves as closely as possible those waters that we have delegated to the contemplation of what exists." [1] But is it the lake or the eye that contemplates best? A lake, a pool, still water – each makes us stop at its edge. It tells the will: you shall not pass; you have to go back to looking at distant things, things beyond! While you were running, something here was already looking. A lake is a great tranquil eye. A lake absorbs all the light and makes a world of it. The world is already contemplated, already represented by the lake. The lake, too, can say: the world is my representation. Near a lake, we understand the old physiological theory of *active vision*. For the active vision, it seems that the eye projects light and illuminates its images itself. We understand how the eye might have the will to see its visions, how contemplation might also be an act of will.

The cosmos, in some way, has a touch of narcissism. The world wants to see itself. The will, considered in its Schopenhauerian aspect, creates eyes in order to contemplate, to feed upon beauty. Is not the eye itself a luminous beauty? Does it not bear the mark of pancalism? [2] It must be beautiful in order to see beauty. The iris of the eye must have a beautiful color so that beautiful colors may enter the pupil. Without blue eyes, how may we really see the blue sky? Without black eyes, how may we look at the night? Conversely, all beauty is ocellated. Innumerable poets have felt this pancalistic union of the visible and of vision, have experienced it without defining it. It is a basic law of imagination. For instance, Shelley writes in *Prometheus Unbound*:

1   Paul Claudel, *L'Oiseau noir dans le soleil levant* [Paris: Gallimard, 1929], p. 230.
2   [French *pancalisme*, from the Greek *pan* (everything) and *kalos* (beautiful); a doctrine that claims that beauty is the highest value.]

As a violet's gentle eye
Gazes on the azure sky
Until its hue grows like what it beholds. [3]

What better example could we find of the material imagination at its task of substantive mimicry?

This composite of cosmic narcissism and dynamic pancalism did not escape Victor Hugo's notice. He saw that nature forces us to contemplate. Evoking one of the great scenes of the banks of the Rhine, he wrote: "It was one of those places where that magnificent peacock we call nature seems to strut before our eyes." [4] We can thus say that the peacock is a microcosm of universal pancalism.

And so, in the most diverse forms, on the most varied occasions, in the works of authors most alien to each other, we see an endless exchange recurring between vision and the visible. Everything that makes us see, sees. Lamartine writes in "Graziella": "Lightning flashes ceaselessly through the cracks of my shutters, like the blinking of a fiery eye on the walls of my room." [5] Thus the flash that illuminates, looks.

But if things should look at us somewhat softly, somewhat gravely, pensively – that is the look of water. The study of imagination leads us to this paradox: in the imagination of generalized vision, water plays an unexpected role. The true eye of the earth is water. Within our eyes, it is *water* that dreams. Are not our eyes equivalent to "that unexplored pool of liquid light that God placed in the depths of ourselves"? [6] In nature as well, it is water that sees, water that dreams. "The lake made the garden. Everything takes form around this water that thinks." [7] Once we give ourselves completely to the realm of imagination, with all the combined forces of dream and contemplation, we understand the profundity of Claudel's observation:

3   Percy Bysshe Shelley, Œuvres complètes, trans. Félix Rabbe, [vol. II (Paris: Stock, 1908), p. 223. Prometheus Unbound (Seattle: University of Washington Press, 1959), p. 293].
4   Victor Hugo, Le Rhin, vol. II [Paris: J. Hetzel and Quentin, 1891], p. 20.
5   Alphonse de Lamartine, Confidences [Paris: Hachette, 1900], p. 247.
6   Claudel, L'Oiseau noir, p. 229.
7   Ibid.

Thus water is the eye of the earth, its apparatus for looking at time. [8]

The Reciprocity of Dream and Work

TV: 92–93

If, passively, as an idle visitor, you find yourself in the stifling atmosphere surrounding a china kiln, then the *anguish of heat* takes hold
of you. [9] You retreat. You do not want to look any longer. You are
afraid of the sparks. You think it is hell.

Nevertheless, move closer. Take on in your imagination the work
of the artisan. Imagine yourself putting the wood into the oven:
cram the oven with shovels full of coal, challenge the oven to a duel
of energy. In short, be ardent and the ardor of the hearth will shoot
its arrows in vain against your chest; you will be invigorated by the
struggle. The fire can only return your blows. The psychology of
opposition invigorates the worker. "How I envied the workers who
served this purifying oven!" says Carossa. "Against them, against
the active, it has apparently no power."

To participate no longer in heat as a state but in heat as growth, to
assist enthusiastically the becoming of its growth – its active, quali-
fying quality – grants immunity against the very excesses of fire.
The worker is no longer the servant of fire, he is its master.

Therefore the passionate worker, enriched with all the dynamic
values of the dream, experiences the dynamic time of the firing. He
willingly, actively, completes the *destiny of the paste*. [10] It was soft and

8   Ibid.
9   [At the beginning of this section, Bachelard indicates that he will comment on passages from Hans Carossa's *Les Secrets de la maturité* (Paris: Stock,
1940), pp. 79–90, which describe a visit to a china factory in Bohemia.]
10   [Bachelard gives to the word *pâte* a very broad meaning: paste represents
any malleable matter (dough, clay, molten metal); it acquires the value of a
central and direct metaphor of imaginary life – as do the tree and the flame.
Bachelard has already treated this theme in several passages of ER (19, 142–52);
he comes back to it in PR (144–45). Paste is not only an example of material
combination (earth and water), it also provides the occasion for any creative
transformation. Kneading and modeling are paradigms of reverie and spiri-

malleable when he encountered it. He wants it to be firm and true. He follows the abrupt yet cautious advance of a fire that gently, powerfully, seizes the piece from all sides. In the span of each firing he relives the entire story of Bernard Palissy. [11] He may not have read it; but he knows it. His experience is an interweaving of dream and dexterity. It is a convergence of natural forces. What was born in water is completed in fire. Earth, water, and fire cooperate in the creation of an everyday object. In a parallel way, great elemental dreams unite themselves in an innocent soul and give it the grandeur of a demiurge.

Take away dreams and you stultify the worker. Leave out the oneiric forces of work and you diminish, you annihilate the artisan. Each labor has its oneirism, each material worked on contributes its inner reveries. Respect for deep psychological forces must lead us to keep the oneirism of work safe from any harm. We can accomplish nothing good against our will, that is to say, against our dreams. The oneirism of work is the very condition of the worker's mental integrity.

The Cogito of Kneading

TV: 78–80

Putting aside all question of the mixture of earth and water, it seems possible to affirm the existence, in the realm of material imagination, of a true prototype of *imaginary paste*. In the imagination of each of us there exists the material image of an ideal paste, a perfect synthesis of resistance and malleability, a marvelous equilibrium between accepting forces and refusing forces. Starting from this equilibrium, which gives an immediate eagerness to the working hand, there arise opposing pejorative judgments: *too soft* or *too hard*. One could say as well that midway between these contrary extremes,

---

tual life. "The space in which the dreamer is immersed is a 'plastic mediator' between man and the universe" (PR: 144). While provoking our creative energy, paste also stimulates our consciousness and thus gives rise to an intense happiness.]

11 [French potter, 1510–1589 or 1590, who experimented with ceramics. After sixteen years of effort he produced a pure white enamel and became known for the fine colored glazes of his wares.]

the hand recognizes instinctively the perfect paste. A normal material imagination immediately places this optimum paste into the hands of the dreamer. Everyone who dreams of paste knows this perfect mixture, as unmistakable to the hand as the perfect solid is to the geometrician's eye. D'Annunzio noted, as a poet, the constitution of this *balanced*, inner paste: the baker, "after testing the dough, poured a little more water into the kneading-trough to thin out the mixture; his hand was so steady measuring the proportions, so deft in tilting the pitcher, that I saw the clear water tracing a perfect, unbroken crystal arc from the lip of the pottery to the flour." [12] It is because the dough is moistened precisely that the picture is so precisely drawn; the water falls into the kneading trough in a geometric curve. Material beauty and formal beauty attract each other. The perfect paste is therefore the original element of materialism, as the perfect solid is the original, formal element of geometry. Any philosopher who rejects this primitivity fails to penetrate materialistic philosophy.

The reality of this dream of the perfect paste goes so deep in us, the convictions that it produces are so profound, that we may speak of a *cogito* of kneading. Philosophers have taught us to extend the Cartesian *cogito* to experiences other than thought. They mention in particular Maine de Biran's *cogito*, in which the being finds proof of his existence in the very act of his effort. To Maine de Biran, the consciousness of activity is as immediate as the consciousness that one is a thinking being. But we must select the most beautiful experiences from among felicitous efforts. The phenomenology of opposition is one of the approaches that give us a better understanding of the mutual involvement of subject and object. But does not the effort yield its most convincing proofs, somehow multiplied, when a being acts upon itself? Here then is the *cogito* of kneading in its narrowest association: there is a way of clenching the fist so that our own flesh is revealed as this elemental, perfect paste that at the same time resists and yields. To the Stoics, the geometry of the open and

12   Gabriele d'Annunzio, *Le Dit du sourd et du muet*, [in *Prose di Ricerca*, vol. III (Verona: Mondadori, 1956), pp. 557–58].

of the closed hand disclosed symbols of meditation. To the philosopher who does not hesitate to draw proofs of his being from his very dreams, the dynamics of a clenched fist – closed neither violently nor gently – gives him both his being and his world ...

If the dreaming man can have such beautiful impressions, should we be surprised if the material and dynamic imagination has at its disposition a sort of *essential paste*, a *primal clay* well suited for *receiving* and *keeping* the forms of all things? Such a material image, so simple, so intense, so alive, is naturally an easy prey to concepts. That is the fate of all fundamental images. And the concept of a paste that is deformed before our eyes is so clear and so general that it makes participation in the original dynamic image useless. Visual images then regain their primacy. The eye – that inspector – prevents us from working.

If poetry is to revive forces of creation in the soul, if it is to help us to relive our natural dreams in all their intensity and all their functions, we must understand that the hand, as well as the eye, has its reveries and its poetry. We therefore have to discover the poems of touch, the poems of the modeling hand.

The Law of Ambivalence

ER: 16–17

... There are profound and durable ambivalences inherent in the fundamental matters that material imagination draws upon. This psychological property is so constant that we can formulate its converse as a basic law of imagination: *a matter to which the imagination cannot give twofold life cannot play the psychological role of a fundamental substance.* A matter that does not elicit a psychological ambivalence cannot find its poetic double that allows endless transpositions. It is necessary then to have a double participation – participation of desire and fear, participation of good and evil, peaceful participation of black and white – for the material element to involve the entire soul.

TR: 82–83

... In the realm of imagination there is no value without polyvalence. The ideal image must seduce us through all our senses and draw us beyond the sense that is most clearly committed. Such is the secret of correspondences that invite us to the multiple life, to the metaphorical life. Sensations then are nothing more than the occasional cause of *isolated images*. The *real cause* of the flow of images is actually the *imagined cause* ...

A dialectic of values actuates the *imagination* of qualities. To imagine a quality is to give it a value that goes beyond or contradicts the sensible value, the real value. We show imagination when we elaborate on sensation, when we break away from coarse impressions (colors or odors) and glorify shadings and bouquets. We seek the *other* in the midst of the *identical*.

Perhaps this philosophy might become clearer if we posed the problem of the imagination of qualities from the point of view of literary imagination. We can easily find examples in which *one sense* is stimulated by *another sense*. Sometimes a substantive is sensualized by two contrary adjectives. In the realm of imagination, what could be the possible use of a noun provided with a single adjective? Would not the adjective in that case be immediately absorbed in the noun? How could the adjective resist this absorption? What does the single adjective do other than weigh upon the noun? To say that a carnation is red is only to designate a *red carnation*. A rich language would say that with a single word. Confronted with a red carnation, we shall thus need more than the word *carnation* and the word *red* put together to express the whinnying of its red fragrance. Who will tell us of this brutality? Who will arouse the sadism and masochism of our imagination at the sight of this bold flower? [13]

---

13   [See also the selection entitled "The secret of milk."]

The Totality of the Root Image

TR: 290–92, 299–305

Primary images have a philosophical advantage: by studying them, we may examine in connection with each of them practically all the problems of a metaphysics of imagination. The image of the root is particularly suitable in this respect. In Jung's thought it corresponds, like the image of the serpent, to an archetype buried in the unconscious of all races; it has, in the clearest part of the mind and even at the level of abstract thought, a potential for multiple metaphors that remain simple and always understood ...

Considered as a *dynamic image*, the root assumes the most diverse powers. It is both a sustaining force and a terebrant force. At the border of two worlds, the air and the earth, the image of the root is animated paradoxically in two directions, depending on whether we dream of a root bearing to heaven the juices of the earth, or of a root going to work among the dead, for the dead ... A root is always a discovery. We dream it more than we see it.

It surprises us when we discover it: is it not rock and hair, flexible filament and hard wood? With it, we have an example of contradictions among things. In the realm of imagination, the dialectic of contraries proceeds through *objects*, by opposition of differentiated, reified substances. How we would activate the imagination if we were to seek out systematically *objects* that contradict each other! We would then see great images like the root accumulate contradictions of *objects*. Negation then operates between things, not merely between acceptance and refusal of the functioning of a verb. Images are primary psychic realities. In experience itself, everything begins with images.

The root is the mysterious tree, it is the subterranean, inverted tree. For the root, the darkest earth – like the pond, but without the pond – is also a mirror, a strange opaque mirror that doubles every aerial reality with a subterranean image. By this reverie, the philosopher writing these pages tells clearly in what a superabundance of dark metaphors he may be involved while dreaming of roots. His excuse is that he has quite often found in his reading the image of a tree growing upside down, whose roots, like a delicate foliage, tremble in the subterranean winds while its branches take root firmly in the blue sky.

I believe that there are objects that have integrative powers, things that enable us to incorporate images. For me, the tree is an *integrating object*. It is normally a work of art. Thus, when I managed to confer upon the tree's aerial psychology the complementary concern with roots, a new life suffused the dreamer in me; the line generated a stanza, the stanza a poem. One of the greatest verticals of man's imaginary life took on the full range of its inductive dynamism. The imagination then took possession of all the powers of plant life. To live like a tree! What growth! What depth! What uprightness! What truth! Immediately, within us, we feel the roots working, we feel that the past is not dead, that we have something to do today in our dark, subterranean, solitary, aerial life. The tree is everywhere at once. The old root – in the imagination there are no young roots – will produce a new flower. The imagination is a tree. It has the integrative virtues of a tree. It is root and boughs. It lives between earth and sky. It lives in the earth and in the wind. The imagined tree becomes imperceptibly the cosmological tree, the tree that epitomizes a universe, that makes a universe ... [14]

However, in order to demonstrate more clearly the value of this power of integration, I shall first give an example of a sickly soul, of a *sickly image*, which we would like to heal by integration into a total image: a kind of root that has lost its tree.

I take this image from Jean-Paul Sartre's *Nausea*. I shall use the passage I am transcribing to bring out the "botanical diagnosis" of an imaginary life:

> So, I was in the park just now. The roots of the chestnut tree were sunk in the ground, just under my bench. I couldn't remember it was a root any more. The words had vanished, and with them, tbe significance of things, their methods of use, and the feeble points of reference that

14   See "L'arbre aérien," *L'Air et les songes*, [pp. 231–55].

> men have traced on their surface. I was sitting, stooping
> forward, head bowed, alone in front of this black, knotty
> mass, entirely beastly, which frightened me. [15]

Since he is so busy showing the sudden obliteration of a world,
Sartre does not describe in enough detail this sort of fascination by
disappearance that attracts the dreamer at the very moment when
he is giving himself up to the inner newness of the root. Beneath the
surface, beneath the roughness, beneath the patched cloak of barks
and fibers, there circulates a paste: "This root was kneaded into existence." And what defines the universe of nausea what identifies
a *nauseous vegetality*, is that beneath the solid crust and the "boiled
leather" of the membranes one experiences the *existence* of the root
as the existence of "soft, monstrous masses, all in disorder – naked,
in a frightful, obscene nakedness." How indeed could this nauseous,
flabby nakedness help being obscene?

Along with this completely passive participation in soft interiors,
images proliferate – especially those metaphors that continue the
strange metamorphosis of hardness into softness, of the hard root
into a soft paste. The dreamer is on the way to a transcendence of absurdity. Absurdity is normally a concept of the intellect; how can we
reconstitute it in the very realm of the imagination? Sartre shows us
how things are absurd before ideas. "The word absurdity is coming
to life under my pen; a little while ago, in the garden, I couldn't find
it, but neither was I looking for it, I didn't need it: I thought without
words, on things, with things." [16] We must add that the dreamer
was himself a *continuum of images*: "Absurdity was not an idea in
my head, or the sound of a voice, only this long serpent dead at my
feet, this wooden serpent. Serpent or claw or root or vulture's talon,
what difference does it make." To participate through reverie in the
text, we may replace the conjunction *or* with the conjunction *and*.
The *or* departs from the fundamental laws of oneiric life. In the unconscious, *or* does not exist. Moreover, the very fact that the author

15   Jean-Paul Sartre, *La Nausée* [Paris: Gallimard, 1938], p. 161. [*Nausea*, trans.
Lloyd Alexander (New York: New Directions, 1964), pp. 126–27.]
16   [This and the following quotations in this passage are taken from *Nausea*,
p. 129.]

adds "what difference does it make" is proof that his dream is not affected by the dialectic of the serpent and the vulture. In conclusion let us add that in the oneiric world there is no such thing as a dead snake. The snake is *cold* movement, the horrible *living cold*. After these slight corrections, let us study the oneirism of the Sartrean root in its syncretism and its special life. Let us consider it as a *total dream* that shapes together the existence of the dreamer and the existence of the image.

The root of the chestnut tree becomes absurd in relation to an entire universe, and first of all to its immediate phenomena. "Absurd: in relation to the stones, the tufts of yellow grass, the dry mud, the tree ..." Absurd to the tree and to the earth: that is the double sign that gives such a special meaning to the Sartrean root. Of course, in this complete adherence to a particular oneiric intuition, the dreamer has long since become detached from the functions taught by elementary botany: "I saw clearly that you could not pass from its function as a root, as a breathing pump, to that, to this hard and compact skin of a sea lion, to this oily, callous, headstrong look." We need not insist: "It is a root," the power of metaphors is too great, the bark has long been a skin because the wood is flesh; the skin is oily because the flesh is soft. Nausea oozes everywhere. Real words no longer form obstacles, no longer can they stop the somnambulistic images that take an extraordinary direction. Absurdity is now universal because the images have been turned from their source, bringing confusion to the very center of the *material imagination.*

It is perhaps through a detailed examination of the sluggish somnambulism of this root that we may best reveal the slowing down of the state of nausea. The root is a serpent and a claw; but it is a serpent that winds torpidly, a claw that unclenches, a claw that is no longer the subject of the verb to claw. The image of the root that takes the earth in its grip and that of the serpent that slithers into the ground, swifter in its twistings than a straight arrow – images that we have studied in their traditional dynamism [17] – here are both *slackened.*

17   [In TR a chapter devoted to images of the serpent precedes the chapter on the root.]

I wanted merely to present a curious and aberrant type of root image. I have done an injustice to Sartre's text in isolating one of its images, which is only a perspective on a vast *Anschauung*. And the cosmos of *Nausea*, particularly in the garden scene, with the trees, with those great "awkward bodies" pursuing the root's limp penetration into the soil, involves any attentive reader in a world characterized in depth.

The Forge: Expansion to the Cosmic Level

TV: 156–59, 163–64

... The forge is one of the great reveries of the will in literature. Can the literary tableau observed in the village forge have a broader illustration? For example, when a fanatic dreamer sees the sun setting on the anvil of the horizon, will he take a legendary hammer to strike the last sparks from the incandescent block?

At this point, I will make a confession about the history of my research. In working on the problems of imagination, I had seen that it would be interesting to study systematically the amplification of literary images to the cosmic level. It was while tracing this habitual cosmic growth of images that I asked the above question, which became for me a veritable *reading hypothesis*. In spite of abundant and varied reading – necessarily thorough, since I am seeking the image in its particularity – my hypothesis renamed in abeyance for years. It seemed useless to me, it seemed born of a mere personal fancy that had no right to appear in this collection of objective reveries I was trying to organize. And yet how many setting suns, how many bleeding, slaughtered suns I have seen in my reading! Never have I felt so clearly the validity of the article in which Gabriel Audisio decries the excess of blood images in contemporary literature.

But one day a fortunate reading brought me confirmation of the hypothesis of the evening forge. The image is sketched in *Tess of the d'Urbervilles*, where Thomas Hardy sees "the sun settled down upon the levels, with the aspect of a great forge in the heavens." [18] In

18   Thomas Hardy, *Tess d'Urberville*, vol. I, [trans. Madeleine Rolland (Paris:

The Woodlanders Hardy uses the image again: "She looked toward the western sky, which was now aglow like some vast foundry wherein new worlds were being cast." [19] After this, my documentation grew little by little. The poetry of the *tormented* dawn, which appears in so many passages of Mary Webb's works, is expressed in a similar image: "Vast black clouds shaped like anvils for some terrific smithy work, were ranged round the horizon, and, later, the east glowed like a forge." [20] A Russian poet, Maximilian Voloshin, says in a single verse, without completing the image:

> Where the blows of a hammer have forged dawns.

José Corti, in an early poem, develops the image further:

> Like a block of iron beaten on the anvil,
> the sun grows thinner under the repeated blows
> of unknown Titans that, far away, in the mist,
> forge beams of light for the sunset.

The image suggests itself as well to a Provençal poet:

> You would think ...
> that fantastic smiths
> were pounding on the red sun. [21]

Once a primal image has been identified, we can no longer ignore its profound and cosmic life; it is in the fullness of nature that human imagination wants to play its role. We no longer need a colorful imagery or clearly defined forms to experience a growing image that acquires a cosmic and mythical value. Is it not somehow a *myth of an aerial Vulcan* that gives deep resonance to a stanza by Loys Masson in his "Prayer to Milosz": "I closed your book, and suddenly it was as if

Hachette, 1924)], p. 237. [*Tess of the d'Urbervilles* (London: Harper and Brothers, 1935), p. 229.]

19   Thomas Hardy, *Les Forestiers*, [trans. Antoinette Six (Paris: Nouvelle Librairie française, 1932)], p. 98. [*The Woodlanders* (London: Macmillan and Co., 1920), pp. 78–79.]

20   Mary Webb, *La Renarde*, [trans. Marie Canavaggia and Jacques de Lacretelle (Paris: Catalogne et Cie, 1935)], p. 369. [*Gone to Earth* (London: Jonathan Cape, 1933), p. 288.]

21   Théodore Aubanel, "Li Fabre," [in *Œuvres choisies* (Avignon: Edouard Aubanel, 1961), p. 130].

you had given me an amber hammer, and with the amber hammer of the Northern clouds I made the tropical evening resound." [22]

This poetic image may seem obscure. Indeed, it needs to be developed, in the photographic sense of the term, by the original image of the hammered sunset, of the orient in the forge. Then, the reader's reverie becomes sensitive to hidden tonalities, it discovers the infinite depths of the imagining soul. To produce this image, the poet has set in motion multiple powers that cover several regions of the unconscious. The image of the amber hammer striking the clouds is not an ephemeral image, not an arrangement of visions offered by sights merely contemplated. The active storm is summoned to work as a being.

When, through imagination, the setting sun has been forged on the horizon, we can better understand the reverie of a subterranean forge; we thus have at our disposal one more image for the analysis of the myths of Vulcan. There are mythologists who tell us that volcanoes are the origin of Vulcan's forges. But volcanoes are too scarce to arouse so many reveries involving subterranean forges. And perhaps it is better to listen to the mythologist who re-imagines than to the mythologist who knows. In the synopsis of the fifth book of *Orpheus*, Ballanche says: "The island of Lemnos had a volcano, which is why Vulcan's forges were said to be there; but this is mythology after the fact. Spontaneous mythology, like Homer's, locates Vulcan's forges in the sky." [23]

Finally, the sun setting on the mountains can provide images of a universe at work. We need not search, as Jean-Pierre Rossignol proposed, in regions "rich in iron" for "the deities of functions that require violent movement and great noise." [24]

---

22 ["A Milosz," in *Loys Masson*, ed. Charles Moulin (Paris: Seghers, Collection Poètes d'aujourd'hui, 1962), p. 101.]
23 [Pierre-Simon Ballanche, *Orphée*, in *Essais de palingénesie sociale*, vol. II (Paris: Didot, 1829). Although Ballanche wrote an *Orphée* in eight books, Bachelard seems to be incorrect in suggesting that he also wrote a synopsis of the work.]
24 Jean-Pierre Rossignol, *Les Métaux dans l'Antiquité* [Paris: A. Durand], 1863, p. 9.

Noise, force, grandeur – in short, the cosmic nature of images is the result of the imaginary life's tendency to magnify. One who dreams of the forge will never need a volcano to hear the subterranean hammers, nor a real mine to have a universe to forge.

I have collected sufficient images on a certain type of setting sun. I would be giving a false impression of imagination if I did not insist on the scarcity of these images. They have been gathered in the course of considerable study, and the reader would be justified in seeing the mania of a collector in the fact that I have considered only this rare image. In fact, the setting sun is an image of nirvana, an image of peace, of acceptance of nocturnal life; and as such, this image of the sun stretching, spreading out, of the sun associating its own repose with the entire universe, dominates a vast area of the reverie of evening. But it is in a doctrine of *anti-nirvana*, such as the doctrine of dynamic imagination that I am presenting, that this image of the sun, which a thoughtful, forceful worker hammers on the hill, takes on unusual significance. The dreamer seems to be forcing the sun to crash, to bury itself. Absorbed in his cosmic dream, the dreamer ends his day by becoming conscious that his force dominates the universe.

The Chamber of a Dream

TR: 52–54

Sometimes, in a great poet's work, a dialectic of inwardness and expansion takes so subdued a form that we forget the dialectic of the large and the small, which is nonetheless the basic one. In this case, the imagination no longer delineates, it transcends delineated forms and it develops *exuberantly* the values of *inwardness*. In sum, any inner richness expands limitlessly the interior space in which it is condensed. The dream withdraws into this interior pace and develops in the most paradoxical delight, in the most ineffable happiness. Let us follow Rilke in his search for a sweetly intimate *body* in the heart of the rose:

> What skies are mirrored
> within the inner lake
> of these open roses.

The whole sky is contained within the space of a rose. The world lives within a fragrance. The intensity of an inner beauty condenses the beauties of an entire universe. Then, in a second movement, the poem expresses the expansion of beauty. These roses

> ... can barely stand by themselves;
> many, swollen to the point of bursting,
> overflow with inner space
> into days that enclose an ever vaster fullness,
> until the entire summer becomes a chamber,
> a chamber within a dream. [25]

The entire summer is *in* a flower; the rose overflows with inner space. At the level of objects, the poet makes us experience the two directions so grossly labeled by psychoanalysts as introversion and extroversion. These directions correspond so well to the poem's inspiration that we may profit by following them in their evolution. The poet is looking for both inwardness and images. He wishes *to express the interiority of a being of the external world.* He does it with a strange purity of abstraction, withdrawing from immediate images, conscious that one does not arouse dreams by describing. He confronts us with the simplest motives of reverie with him, we enter *the chamber of a dream.*

The Rehabilitation of the Wardrobe Image

PE: 79–80, 83–84

I always feel a slight shock, a certain mild, philological pain, whenever a great writer uses a word in a derogatory sense. To begin with, all words do an honest job in our everyday language, and not even the most ordinary among them, those that are attached to the most common-

---

25 Rainer Maria Rilke, "Interieur de la rose," [*Poèsies*, trans. Maurice Betz (Paris: Emile Paul 1938], p. 14. ["Das Rosen-Innere," *Sämtliche Werke*, vol. I (Leipzig: Insel Verlag, 1955), p. 622.]

place realities, lose their poetic possibilities as a result of this fact. But somehow, when Bergson uses the word "drawer," he does it disdainfully. Indeed, the word always appears in the role of a controversial metaphor, giving orders and passing judgment, always in the same way. Our philosopher dislikes compartmented arguments.

This seems to me to be a good example for demonstrating the radical difference between image and metaphor. I shall therefore insist upon this difference before returning to my examination of the images of intimacy that are in harmony with drawers and chests, as also with all the other hiding places in which human beings, great dreamers of locks, keep or hide their secrets.

Although there is a superabundance of metaphor in Bergson's writings, in the last analysis, his images are rare. It is as though, for him, imagination were entirely metaphorical. Now a metaphor gives concrete substance to an impression that is difficult to express. Metaphor is related to a psychic being from which it differs. An image, on the contrary, product of absolute imagination, owes its entire being to the imagination. Later, when I plan to go more deeply into the comparison between metaphor and image, we shall see that metaphor could not be studied phenomenologically, and that in fact, it is not worth the trouble, since it has no phenomenological value. At the moment, it is a *fabricated image*, without deep, true, genuine roots. It is an ephemeral expression. It is, or should be, one that is used only once, in passing. We must be careful, therefore, not to give it too much thought; nor should the reader think too much about it. And yet, what a success the drawer metaphor has had with Bergson's followers!

Contrary to metaphor, we can devote our reading being to an image since it confers being upon us. In fact, the image, which is the pure product of absolute imagination, is a phenomenon of being; it is also one of the specific phenomena of the speaking creature ...

Wardrobes with their shelves, desks with their drawers, and chests with their false bottoms are veritable organs of the secret psychological life. Indeed, without these "objects" and a few others in equally high favor, our intimate life would lack a model of intimacy. They are hybrid objects, subject objects. Like us, through us and for us, they have a quality of intimacy ...

Bergson did not want the faculty of memory to be taken for a wardrobe of recollections. But images are more demanding than ideas. And the most Bergsonian of his disciples, being a poet, recognized that memory is a wardrobe. The following great line was written by Charles Péguy:

> On the shelves of memory and in the temples
> of the wardrobe. [26]

But the real wardrobe is not an everyday piece of furniture. It is not opened every day, and so, like a heart that confides in no one, the key is not on the door.

> The wardrobe had no keys! ... No keys had the big wardrobe
> Often we used to look at its brown and black door
> No keys! ... It was strange! Many a time we dreamed
> Of the mysteries lying dormant between its wooden flanks
> And we thought we heard, deep in the gaping lock
> A distant sound, a vague and joyful murmur. [27]

Here Rimbaud designates a perspective of hope: what good things are being kept in reserve in the locked wardrobe? This time it is filled with promise, it is something more than a family chronicle.

André Breton, with a single word, show's us the marvels of unreality by adding a blessed impossibility to the riddle of the wardrobe. In *Revolver aux cheveux* blancs he writes with typical surrealist imperturbability:

> The wardrobe is filled with linen
> There are even moonbeams, which I can unfold. [28]

---

26 "Aux rayons de mémoire et aux temples de l'armoire." Quoted by Albert Béguin in L'"Eve" de Péguy (Paris: Labergerie, 1948), p. 49.

27 Arthur Rimbaud, "Les Étrennes des orphelins," [in Œuvres, ed. Suzanne Bernard (Paris: Garnier, 1960), p. 37].

28 "L'armoire est pleine de linge / Il y a même des rayons de lune que je peux déplier." [André Breton, Revolver aux cheveux blancs (Paris: Éditions des Cahiers Libres, 1932), p. 110.]

Another poet, Joseph Rouffange (Deuil et luxe du cœur [Paris: Rougerie, 1963]) writes:
In the dead linen in cupboards
I seek the supernatural.

This carries the image to a point of exaggeration that no reasonable mind would care to attain. But exaggeration is always at the summit of any living image. And to add fantasy linen is to draw a picture, by means of a volute of words, of all the superabundant blessings that lie folded in piles between the flanks of an abandoned wardrobe. How big, how enveloping, is an old sheet when we unfold it. And how white the old tablecloth was, white as the moon on the wintry meadow! If we dream a bit, Breton's image seems perfectly natural.

The Permanent Childhood

PR: 85–87, 92, 106–7

All the ideas that I want to put forth in this chapter tend to establish the persistence in the human soul of a nucleus of childhood, of a motionless but enduring childhood, outside of history, hidden from others, disguised as history when it is narrated but having real existence only in its moments of illumination – which is to say in its moments of poetic existence.

While the child was dreaming in solitude, it experienced a limitless existence. Its reverie was not merely an escape. It was a reverie of flight.

The dream – being passes through all the ages of humankind, from childhood to old age, without growing old. And that is why, later in life, one experiences a sort of double reverie when one attempts to revive childhood dreams ...

Dreaming of childhood, we go back to the den of reveries, to the reveries that opened up the world for us. It is reverie that makes us the first inhabitants of the world of solitude. And we live all the better in the world, living as the solitary child lives in images. In the child's reverie, the image comes first. Experiences only come afterward; they go against the current of all reveries of flight. The child's vision is grand and beautiful. Reverie oriented toward childhood takes us back to the beauty of first images.

The child knows a natural reverie of solitude that we must not con-
fuse with that of the sulky child. In his happy solitude, the dreaming
child experiences cosmic reverie – that reverie thatunites us with
the world.

In my opinion, it is in the memories of this cosmic solitude that
we must find the nucleus of childhood that remains at the center of
the human psyche. That is where imagination and memory are most
closely interwoven. That is where the childhood being weaves together the real and the imaginary, and lives in the fullness of imagination the images of reality. All these images of his cosmic solitude
react in depth within the being of the child; separated from its being for humankind, there is created, under the world's influence,
a being for the world. [29] That is the being of cosmic childhood.
Humankind passes by, the cosmos remains, an ever-primal cosmos
that the greatest sights of the world will never efface through the
entire course of life. The cosmic nature of our childhood remains in
us. It reappears in our solitary reveries. The nucleus of cosmic childhood exists in us therefore as a false memory. Our solitary reveries
are the activities of a metamemory. Our reveries that turn toward
childhood seem to reveal a being pre-existing our own, an entire
perspective of *antecendence of being.*

In these reveries, in the poems that we would all like to write in order to revive our primal reveries and restore the world of happiness,
childhood, to use the terms of depth psychology, appears as a true
archetype, the archetype of simple happiness. It is certainly a focus
of images that attract happy images and repel the experiences of
unhappiness. But this image, in its origins, is not entirely ours; it
has roots that go deeper than mere memories. Our childhood bears
witness to the childhood of humankind, to the being touched by the
glory of living.

From that time on, our personal, clear, and oft-repeated memories can never completely explain why the reveries that carry us
back to our childhood have such an appeal, such value for the soul.

29   [Bachelard forms expressions on the model of Sartre's *l'être-pour-autrui* and
l'être-pour-soi.]

The reason why this value withstands the experiences of life is that childhood remains a source of life deep within us, a life that stays in harmony with the possibilities of new beginnings. Everything that originates in us with the clarity of a new beginning is a mad surge of life. The great archetype of incipient life gives to any beginning the psychic energy that Jung acknowledged in every archetype.

Like the archetypes of fire, water, and light, childhood, which is water, which is fire, which becomes a light, gives rise to a great proliferation of fundamental archetypes. All the archetypes that link man to the world and that provide a poetic harmony between humankind and the universe somehow take on a new life in our reveries of childhood.

I ask the reader not to reject this notion of the *poetic harmony* of archetypes without further examination. I would like so much to show that poetry is a synthesizing force for human existence! As I see them, archetypes are reserves of enthusiasm that help us to believe in the world, to love the world, to create our world. The philosophical theme of the openness onto the world would gain so much more concrete meaning if philosophers read the poets! Every archetype is an opening out, an invitation to the world. Each opening gives rise to a reverie of flight. And reveries direced toward childhood restore to us the powers of primal reveries. The water, fire, trees, and vernal flowers of childhood – what genuine bases for an analysis of the world!

The Oneiric House

TR: 95–96, 98, 104, 110–11

When we go to live in the house of memory, the real world vanishes all at once. What are the houses on our street worth compared to the house of our birth, that house of total interiority that gave us our sense of inwardness? That house is remote, is lost, we no longer live in it, we are only too sure that we will never live in it again. And so it is more than a memory. It is a house of dreams, our oneiric house.

When one knows how to grant to all *things* their exact dream potential, one lives more fully in the oneiric house than in the house of memories. The oneiric house is a deeper theme than that of the house of our birth; it corresponds to a more profound need. If the house of our birth has such foundations in us, it is because it responds to unconscious inspirations that are deeper – more intimate – than the mere concern for preservation, for the retention of initial warmth, for the protection of initial light. The house of memory, the house of our birth, is built over the crypt of the oneiric house. Within the crypt we find the root, the bonds, the depth, the fathomlessness of dreams. We *lose* ourselves in this dimension; it has an infinity. We dream of it as of a desire, an image that we find sometimes in books. Instead of dreaming of what has been, we dream of what should have been, of what would have stabilized forever our inner reveries ...

With the cellar as its root, with the nest on its roof, the complete oneiric house constitutes one of the vertical schemes of human psychology ...

There is no true oneiric house that is not vertically organized: its cellar firmly rooted in the earth, the ground floor for daily life, the upper floor for sleeping, and the attic near the roof. Such a house has everything necessary to symbolize the deep fears, the banality of daily life at ground level, and sublimations at the upper levels. Of course, a complete oneiric topology would require detailed study, and we would have to acknowledge as well, at times, some very odd retreats; a closet, a space beneath the stairs, an old wood shed may indicate suggestive lines for a psychology of confined life. Such a life would have to be studied in the two opposite senses of the dungeon and the retreat. But in my total adherence to the inner life of the house in this study, I will leave aside the tantrums and fears nurtured in a child punished by confinement. I will consider only positive dreams, which come back all through life as impulses to innumerable images. We may therefore give as a general law that every child who shuts himself in desires imaginary life: it seems that the smaller the retreat in which the dreamer confines himself, the greater the dreams. As Yanette Deletang-Tardif writes, "The most enclosed being generates waves." [30] Pierre Loti gives perfect expression to this dialectic of the dreamer with drawing into his solitude and initiating waves of reverie in search of immensity: "When I was still a child, I had little hidden places that represented Brazil for me and in which I really managed to have the impressions and fears of a tropical forest." [31]

A child may be given a deep internal life if we grant him a place of solitude, a corner. Ruskin, in his parents' great dining hall, spent long hours confined in his corner. He speaks at length about this in his reminiscences of childhood. Basically, enclosed and exuberant life are both psychic necessities. But before being abstract formulas, they must be psychological realities, with a setting and a decor. These two existences require both the house and the open fields.

Perhaps we may sense now the difference in oneiric richness between the country house, really built on the soil, surrounded by a fence, in its own universe, and the building in which we use a few pigeonholes as residence, standing on nothing but the pavement of the cities. Can we call this a cellar, this tile-floored room piled up more with cases than with barrels?

Thus a philosopher of imagination also faces the problem of "the return to the soil." [32]

30 Yanette Deletang-Tardif, Edmond Jaloux [Paris: Table Ronde, 1947], p. 34.
31 Pierre Loti, Fleurs d'ennui. Suleima [Paris: Calmann-Lévy, 1934], p. 353.
32 [In PS: 28 Bachelard describes his technique for resisting the artificiality of city life. He naturalizes disturbing noises, training himself to hear the ocean when the tumult of the street is too loud. In other passages, Bachelard completes his phenomenology of the refuge by studying homologous image, such as the nest and the shell. The nest, for example, reveals that "being starts with well-being" (PS: 104). He also enriches the dialectics of the house: "We all have our cottage moments and our palace moments" (PS: 63).]

V

POETRY AS SYNTHESIS
OF HUMAN EXISTENCE

Literature Contains All Art

TV: 95

Clay-modeling, a dream that brings us back to our childhood! It has often been said that the child contains all possibilities. As children, we were painters, modelers, botanists, sculptors, architects, hunters, explorers. What has become of all that?

At the very heart of maturity, however, there is a means of regaining these lost possibilities. A means? What! I might be a great painter? – Yes, you might be a great painter a few hours a day. – I might create masterworks? – Yes, you might create wonderful masterpieces, works that would give *you* the direct joys of wonderment, which would take you back to the happy time when the world was a source of wonder.

That means is literature. One has but to *write* the painted work. One has but to write the statue. Pen in hand – if only we are willing to be sincere – we regain all the powers of youth, we reexperience these powers as they used to be, in their naive assurance, with their rapid, linear, sure joys. Through the channel of *literary imagination*, all the arts are ours. A beautiful adjective, well placed, in the right light, sounding in the proper harmony of vowels, is all we need for a substance. A stylistic trait is enough for a personality, for a man. Speaking, writing! Telling, narrating! Inventing the past! Remembering, pen in hand, with the acknowledged and evident intention *to write well, to compose, to make beautiful*, in order to be quite sure that we go beyond the autobiography of a real past event and that we rediscover the autobiography of lost possibilities, the very dreams, the true, real dreams, which we lived with slow, lingering pleasure. The specific aesthetics of literature is to be found there. Literature functions as a substitute. It restores life to lost possibilities.

Reading as a Dimension of Consciousness

PR: 22–23, 131–32

Reading is a dimension of modern consciousness, a dimension that transposes psychic phenomena already transposed by writing. [1] Written language must be considered as a particular psychic reality. A book is permanent: it is a kind of object present before our eyes. It speaks to us with a repetitive authority that we would not experience in the presence of the author himself. We must read what is written. Moreover, in writing, the author has already made a transposition. He would not *say* what he writes. Whether he admits it or not, he has entered the domain of the written psyche ...

The best proof of a book's specific existence is that it is at once a reality of the virtual and a virtuality of the real. When we read a novel, we are placed in another life that makes us suffer, hope, sympathize, but we retain the complex impression, nevertheless, that our anguish remains under the control of our free will, that our anguish is not radical. An agonizing book can therefore offer a technique for reducing anguish. It provides anguished people with a homeopathy of anguish. But this homeopathy is most effective in a meditative reading, when a literary interest endows the text with values. Then two levels of the psyche are split apart, the reader participates in these two levels, and when he is completely conscious of the *aesthetics of anguish*, he is on the point of discovering its factitiousness. For anguish is artificial: we were meant to breathe freely.

That is why poetry – the highest of aesthetic joys – is beneficial ...

And so, early in the morning, seeing the books piled on my table, I say my voracious reader's prayer to the god of reading: "Give us this day our daily hunger" ...

---

1   [See passage concerning poetry and sublimation in Chapter III.]

In its products and in its producer, reverie can very well acquire the etymological meaning of the word poetic. Reverie gathers being around its dreamer. It gives him the illusion of being more than he is. Thus, over the lessened being of the relaxed state in which reverie is formed, a structure takes shape in a relief that the poet will swell into an augmented being. The philosophical study of reverie evokes shadings of ontology.

This ontology is easily grasped, since it is an ontology of well-being – a well-being commensurate with the being of the one capable of dreaming it. There is no well-being without reverie, no reverie without well-being. We discover by reverie, in the first place, that being is good. A philosopher would say: being is a value.

Must we reject this summary characterization of reverie as happiness under pretext that happiness is a psychologically shallow, meager, childish state – and also that the mere word *happiness* stifles all analysis and drowns psychic life in banality? Poets offer us the shadings of a cosmic happiness that are so numerous and varied that we must say that the world of reverie begins with shading. That is how the daydreamer gains an impression of originality. Through shadings, we grasp the dreamer's experience of the nascent *cogito*.

The *cogito* of thought can wander, wait, choose – the *cogito* of reverie is immediately attached to its object, to its image. The shortest distance of all is the one between the imagining subject and the imagined image. Reverie lives on its initial interest. The subject is astonished to encounter the image in his reverie; indeed, he is amazed, charmed, awakened. Great dreamers are masters of sparkling consciousness. A kind of multiple *cogito* takes on new life in the closed world of a poem. Of course, other powers of consciousness are required to take possession of the poem's totality. But the flash of an image already provides us with an illumination. How often discontinuous reveries give life to the dreaming state! Are not two types of reverie possible, as we either let ourselves flow with the happy sequence of images, or live at the center of an image and feel it radiate forth? A *cogito* is firmly established in the soul of the dreamer living at the center of a radiating image.

Suddenly an image occupies the heart of our imagining being. It seizes us, holds us. It infuses us with being. The *cogito* is won over by an object from the world, which by itself represents the world. The imagined detail is a sharp point that penetrates the reverie and prompts the dreamer to a more concrete meditation. His being is simultaneously the being of the image and his commitment to the astonishing image. The image brings us an illustration of our wonderment. The registers of sensation correspond with and complete one another. In reverie on a simple object we experience a polyvalence of our dreaming being.

A flower, a fruit, a simple familiar object suddenly insists that we think of it, that we dream in its company, that we help it to rise to the level of man's companion. Without poets we could never find the direct objects of our dreamer's cogito. Not all worldly objects are available for poetic reveries. But once a poet has chosen his object, the object itself changes being. It is promoted to the poetical.

What a joy it is, then, to take the poet at his word, to dream with him, to believe what he says, to live in the world that he offers us by placing the world under the sign of an object, of a fruit or a flower from the world.

Artificial Paradises

PR: 145–47

A broader investigation than the present one of the aesthetics of oneirism should consider the study of *paradis artificiels* as they are described by writers and poets. We would have to explore numerous phenomenological lines in order to discover the "I" of the many different states corresponding to different narcotics! They would at least have to be divided into three classes: the "I" of sleep if it exists; the "I" of narcosis if it retains an individual value; and the "I" of reverie, which remains in such a state of vigilance that it can afford the joy of writing.

Who will ever determine the ontological weight of all the imagined "I's"? A poet writes:

> Is it ours, this dream in us,
> I make my way alone and multiplied

am I myself, am I another
are we but imagined beings. [2]

Is there an "I" that subsumes these multiple "I's"? An "I" of all others that has mastery over our entire being, over all our inner beings? Novalis writes: "The supreme task of education is to take possession of one's transcendental self, to be at once the 'I' of one's 'I'." [3]

But what am I seeking in these "artificial paradises" – I, a mere armchair psychologist? Dreams or reveries? Which are the decisive documents for me? Books, nothing but books. Would "artificial paradises" be paradises if they were not written? For us readers, they are readers' paradises.

They were written in order to be read, with the assurance that their poetic value would be the means of communication between the author and the reader. It was in order to write that so many poets experimented with the reveries of opium. But who can tell the respective roles of experience and of art? Edmond Jaloux makes a shrewd remark about Edgar Allan Poe: Poe's opium is an *imagined opium*. Imagined before, reimagined afterward, never described during the experience. Who can tell us the difference between experienced opium and transfigured opium? As for us readers who want not to know but to dream, we must follow the ascent from the experience to the poem. According to Jaloux, "the power of man's imagination is greater than any poison." [4] He also says, speaking of Poe: "He ascribes to the poppy one of the most striking characteristics of his own spirituality." [5]

But here again, cannot the one who experiences psychotropic images find in them the same stimulation as in psychotropic substances? The beauty of images increases their effectiveness. The multiplicity of images assumes the function of uniformity of cause. A poet does not hesitate to devote himself entirely to the effectiveness

2   Géo Libbrecht, *Enchanteur de toi-même: Suivi de légende satanique* (Paris: Seghers, Collection Poèmes choisis, 1952), p. 43.
3   "Die höchste Aufgabe der Bildung ist, sich eines transzendentalen Selbst zu bemächtigen, das Ich seines Ichs zugleich zu sein." Novalis, "Blütenstaub," in *Schriften*, vol. II [Jena: E. Diederichs, 1907], p. 117.
4   Edmond Jaloux, *Edgar Poe et les femmes* (Geneva: Éditions du Milieu du Monde, 1943), p. 125.
5   Ibid., p. 129.

of images. Henri Michaux writes: "No need for opium. Everything is a drug to one who chooses to live on the other side." [6]

And what is a beautiful poem if not folly recast? A little poetic order imposed upon aberrant images? It is maintaining intelligent sobriety in the use – however intensive – of imaginary drugs. Reveries, wild reveries, lead our lives.

The Vertical Axis of Reverie

FC: 56–59

Among the reveries that give us buoyancy, reveries of elevation are the most effective and direct. All upright objects point to a zenith. An upright form rises and carries us off in its verticality. [7] The conquest of a real mountain peak is a sporting feat; the dream goes even higher, it takes us to a zone beyond verticality. Many a dream of flight is born in the emulation of verticality aroused by upright and vertical beings. Near towers and trees a dreamer of heights dreams of the sky. Dreams of height give sustenance to our instinct of verticality, an instinct that is repressed by the needs of everyday, prosaically horizontal life. Vertically – tending reverie is the most liberating of all. There is no surer way of dreaming well than dreaming in another world. But is not the world *above* the most decisive of *other* worlds? May dreams develop in which the above forgets and suppresses the below? Living at the zenith of the upright object, gathering reveries of verticality, we experience a transcendence of being. The image of verticality brings us into the realm of values. In communing through imagination with the verticality of an upright object we experience the beneficial influence of lifting forces, we participate in the hidden fire dwelling in beautiful forms, forms assured of their verticality ...

6   Henri Michaux, Plume [Paris: Gallimard, 1957], p. 68.
7   [When Bachelard was working on the elements, particularly in TV, he associated verticality with solid materials (the tree, the granite pillar, etc.) capable of supporting their movement upward. Here, the axes of reverie are more detached from matter and designate instead the dimensions of space and interior life.]

The simpler their object, the greater the reveries. The flame of the candle on the solitary man's table prefigures all the reveries of verticality. The flame is a valiant and fragile vertical. A breath disturbs it, but it rises up anew. A lifting force restores its magic. "The candle burns high and its purple rears up," says a line by Georg Trakl. [8]

The flame is an inhabited verticality. Any dreamer of flame knows that the flame is alive ... And what a full, what a beautiful moment when the candle burns well! What delicate life in the flame that stretches and tapers out! The values of life and dream then reach their full association.

"A stem of fire! Can we ever know all that gives fragrance?" asks another poet. [9] Yes, the stem of a flame is so upright, so frail, that the flame becomes a flower.

Thus images and things exchange their powers. The entire room of the dreamer of flame possesses an atmosphere of verticality. A gentle but firm dynamic force draws dreams toward the heights. One may well be interested in the inner swirls surrounding the wick, and see in the depth of the flame stirrings where shadow and light struggle. But every dreamer of flame lifts his dream toward the summit. It is there that fire becomes light. Villiers de l'Isle-Adam took as the epigraph for a chapter of his Isis this Arab proverb: "The torch does not illuminate its base."

The greatest dreams are in the heights.

The flame is so fundamentally vertical that, for a dreamer of being, it appears stretched toward the beyond, toward an ethereal non-being. In a poem entitled "Flame" we read:

> Bridge of fire thrown between real and unreal constant
> coexistence of being and non-being ... [10]

To play with being and nonbeing, starting from a trifle, from a flame – perhaps merely an imagined flame – is for a philosopher a beautiful instance of illustrated metaphysics.

8   Anthologie de la poèsie allemande des origines à nos jours, vol. II, [ed. and trans. René Lasne and Georges Rabuse (Paris: Stock, 1942)], p. 109.
9   Edmond Jabès, Les Mots tracent [Paris: Librairie "Les Pas perdus," 1951], p. 15.
10   Roger Asselineau, Poèsies incomplètes (Paris: Debresse, 1959), p. 38.